German Baking

Jürgen Krauss

German Baking

Cakes, tarts, traybakes
and breads from
the Black Forest and beyond

Kyle Books

AN HACHETTE UK COMPANY
WWW.HACHETTE.CO.UK

FIRST PUBLISHED IN GREAT BRITAIN IN 2023 BY KYLE BOOKS,
AN IMPRINT OF OCTOPUS PUBLISHING GROUP LIMITED
CARMELITE HOUSE
50 VICTORIA EMBANKMENT
LONDON EC4Y 0DZ

ISBN: 9781914239885

PUBLISHING DIRECTOR: JUDITH HANNAM
PUBLISHER: JOANNA COPESTICK
EDITOR: VICKY ORCHARD
EDITORIAL ASSISTANT: EMMA HANSON
DESIGN: HELEN BRATBY
PHOTOGRAPHY: MAJA SMEND
FOOD STYLING: LIZZIE HARRIS AND KATIE MARSHALL
PROPS STYLING: TONY HUTCHINSON
PRODUCTION: PETER HUNT

A CATALOGUING IN PUBLICATION RECORD FOR THIS TITLE IS AVAILABLE FROM THE
BRITISH LIBRARY.

PRINTED AND BOUND IN CHINA

10 9 8 7 6 5 4 3

Introduction

Imagine a small, square room. You enter it through the door set close to its left corner. From the doorway, you look through the big window, with a view onto the brook, and a steep, overgrown hillside with the ascending road to the church carved into it. You can also see the bricked-up entrance to a tunnel, a bomb shelter that was never used and is now home to bats. Running below the level of the window and along the left wall nestles a corner bench, the boxes under the seats offer practical storage for newspapers and children's books. Between the bench and the door is the wooden table. It is small, but expandable.

Within this small, square room, propped against the remaining walls you will find a coal-fired oven and an electric stove, a sink and a cupboard. You are in the crowded kitchen of my childhood, where my brother and I played, the whole family ate, I did my homework and my mother cooked and baked. This was the centre of my early childhood in Germany.

In such a close space it is inevitable that everybody gets involved in everybody else's activities, and therefore I am sure that I got my hands into dough as soon as I could stand up, even if I don't have memories of the event.

During the year we would bake cheesecakes, marble cakes, Linzer Torte, but the time everybody in the household looked forward to most of all was Advent. In November we would start making Christmas biscuits together, a hugely fun and messy activity. I remember making glazed shortbread biscuits, decorated with hundreds and thousands. My mother was always kind and let my brother and me do what we wanted, which resulted in completely overworked dough and cookie monstrosities that never really baked all the way through!

My baking continued through my teenage years with occasional Linzer Torte, plum tarts and cheesecakes, but I never thought of making layered cakes or bread. The desire to make bread, specifically bread as it was sold in our neighbour's store, emerged sometime after I had moved to the UK where I found that there were excellent books about breadmaking on the market.

By the time I applied for *The Great British Bake Off,* I was a confident bread-baker and had branched into baking cakes and tarts as well. Unexpectedly, my participation in the show reconnected me strongly to the sweet aspects of my past, and I found myself able to develop recipes for many classic delicacies that our family used to buy from bakeries, as well as the cakes and biscuits we used to make in that small kitchen. Many of those recipes have now become favourites of my family in England. This is what this book is all about.

I invite you to accompany me through the flavours of my life in Germany. I hope you enjoy the journey.

MY MOTHER HOLDING ME. SHE IS STANDING IN THE COURTYARD
WHICH HADN'T CHANGED SINCE SHE WAS A CHILD,
AND WAS ALSO THE PLAYGROUND OF MY CHILDHOOD.

Waffles, pancakes and dumplings

P ancakes were always a quick after-school lunch in my home. Usually we had them savoury, with mushrooms and a white sauce. I won't include the standard pancake recipe here because I trust the reader to have their own great recipe. But there are many related recipes popular in Germany, and the collective word for them is Mehlspeise, food made with flour, and in this chapter, I present some family favourites.

Apfel-Küchle
Apple Fritters

Up until the age of 15 there were no afternoon lessons, and my school didn't have a canteen. Therefore, my brother and I returned home from school hungry between 12.30 and 1.30pm, depending on our timetables. My poor mother did what she could to have lunch ready for us, but sometimes that didn't work out, and Apfel-Küchle was a welcome lunch on those occasions.

The three of us got busy in the kitchen together: one of us would peel and core the apples; one of us would slice the apples and one of us would prepare the batter. A very quick, sweet lunch was prepared in record time.

The apples need to be a bit firm after cooking, so I like to use tart, firm apples like Granny Smith.

serves 4 as a dessert

2 LARGE FIRM, TART APPLES,
SUCH AS GRANNY SMITH

100G PLAIN FLOUR

2 MEDIUM EGGS

1 PINCH SALT

100ML WHOLE MILK

VEGETABLE OIL FOR FRYING

CINNAMON SUGAR FOR SPRINKLING
(page 181)

Peel and core the apples. Cut the apples into slices perpendicular to the core, so that you get apple rings. If you don't have an apple corer, cut the slices first and use a sharp round object, like a piping nozzle, to remove the core from each slice.

To prepare the batter, put flour, eggs, salt and milk into a bowl and mix to form a thick, smooth batter.

Heat some oil in a frying pan over a medium heat, so that the base of the pan is well covered with oil. When hot enough to make pancakes, dip an apple ring in the batter, lift it out with a fork and let some of the excess batter drip off. Then transfer it to the frying pan. Repeat until the frying pan is full. The rings shouldn't touch each other.

Fry on one side for about 4 minutes until golden brown and crisp, then turn the rings over and repeat on the other side.

Serve hot, with a sprinkling of cinnamon sugar.

Striebele
Funnel Cake

These pancakes have many names – Striebele, Strauben, Trichterkuchen, funnel cake (in the USA) – and many regions claim them as their own speciality. The German south-west, where I am from, is one of these regions, and often in German cookbooks they are described as a speciality from Baden. But the idea of pouring batter into hot oil using a funnel seems to have been almost universal, as there are very similar treats like this in India (jalebi) and the Arab world (e.g. zalabia in Algeria and Egypt).

One early childhood memory is of my grandma making them. In her kitchen there was a wood-fired range, and to deep-fry she removed some iron rings from the cooking surface. She had a deep-frying pot that could be inserted into this hole. It sealed off the gaps neatly so that fire and smoke couldn't escape, and the lower part of the pot was immersed in the flames. I always loved those crisp, fragile, irregular treats she made.

makes 6–8

YOU WILL NEED A FUNNEL AND A DEEP-FRYER OR A DEEP FRYING PAN

400G PLAIN FLOUR

1 PINCH SALT

30G CASTER SUGAR

350ML WHOLE MILK

4 MEDIUM EGGS

1 TEASPOON VANILLA BEAN PASTE

30G UNSALTED BUTTER, MELTED

VEGETABLE OIL FOR DEEP-FRYING

ICING SUGAR FOR DUSTING

Sift the flour, salt and sugar into a bowl. Add the milk, eggs and vanilla bean paste. Whisk until you have a smooth batter. Add the melted butter and stir in.

Heat enough oil for deep-frying, in a deep, heavy pan or deep-fryer, making sure it is no more than half full to about 180°C. You can tell that the oil is the correct temperature when air bubbles emerge immediately when dipping a wooden spoon in the oil.

Once the oil is hot, hold the funnel in one hand, with a finger sealing the tip. Ladle 2 to 3 tablespoons into the funnel. Now hold the funnel over the oil and release the finger. Move the funnel in irregular spiral movements to create a lattice of strands that hold together a bit.

Once the underside is light golden, turn over your funnel cake and fry until completely golden. This will take about 1–2 minutes.

Transfer the funnel cake onto kitchen paper to let the fat drip off. Repeat with the remaining batter. Serve sprinkled with icing sugar.

Schoko-Waffeln
Chocolate Waffles

This variation of waffles uses melted chocolate as well as cocoa powder to get a rich chocolate flavour. They were a special treat in our family, and just need a light dusting of icing sugar or a dollop of whipped cream to go with them.

makes about 10, depending on the size of your waffle maker

245G PLAIN FLOUR

30G COCOA POWDER

½ TEASPOON BAKING POWDER

50G CHOCOLATE
(54% or 70% cocoa solids, to taste)

125G UNSALTED BUTTER, CUBED, ROOM TEMPERATURE

1 PINCH SALT

75G CASTER SUGAR

3 MEDIUM EGGS, SEPARATED

1 TEASPOON VANILLA BEAN PASTE

225ML WHOLE MILK, ROOM TEMPERATURE

100ML SPARKLING WATER

ICING SUGAR FOR TOPPING

WHIPPED CREAM TO SERVE

Sift the flour, cocoa powder and baking powder into a bowl and set aside.

Melt the chocolate over a bain-marie. To do this, place the chocolate in a heatproof bowl. Take a saucepan with a smaller diameter than the bowl and add about 3cm of boiling water. Place the bowl with chocolate on the saucepan, making sure the water does not touch the bowl. Stir from time to time. This melts the chocolate slowly.

Put the butter, salt and sugar into a big bowl. Using a hand mixer or the balloon whisk on a stand mixer, whisk until it turns fluffy and changes colour. Whisk the egg yolks and vanilla bean paste into the butter mixture. Add the milk, flour mixture and sparkling water bit by bit, alternating between the three.

Whisk the egg whites to soft peaks. Fold the egg whites into the batter.

Fold the melted chocolate into the batter.

This waffle batter is best used immediately. The cooking time depends on the waffle maker used, but the waffles should be a bit crisp.

Serve with icing sugar or a dollop of whipped cream.

Griess-Schnitten
Semolina Fritters

These have always been a favourite of my brother. My mother would have prepared the loaf of dough while we were at school, and she was ready when we came home at 1pm, exhausted and hungry, to feed us this treat.

The fritters are not very sweet, and the texture can be a bit unusual, but sprinkled with cinnamon sugar and served with apple sauce I am sure you will love them.

The semolina dough can be prepared well in advance.

Line a 500g loaf tin, about 15 x 9cm with baking paper or clingfilm and set aside. This will help create nice rectangular slices.

Place the milk, butter, salt, nutmeg and sugar in a saucepan and bring to the boil. Stir in the semolina and keep stirring until a lump forms. Take the saucepan off the heat and stir in one of the eggs. Transfer the semolina dough to the loaf tin, cover with clingfilm or baking paper and set aside to let it cool completely. The dough will set firm.

When you are ready to cook your fritters, beat the remaining egg and pour it onto a big plate. Spread the breadcrumbs onto a second plate.

Remove the semolina block from the loaf tin and wrapping and cut it into 1cm thick slices.

Heat enough oil to coat the bottom of a frying pan on a medium heat.

Take the semolina fritters one by one, coat them first in egg, then in breadcrumbs, and fry them immediately until deep golden on each side, but not burnt. This should take about 4 minutes per side.

Serve them hot, sprinkled with cinnamon sugar, and with apple sauce on the side. Summer fruit or plum compote goes well, too, and for a more luxurious dessert why not serve them with a scoop of ice cream?

serves 4 as a dessert

500ML WHOLE MILK

20G UNSALTED BUTTER

1 PINCH SALT

¼ TEASPOON GROUND NUTMEG

40G CASTER SUGAR

125G FINE SEMOLINA

2 MEDIUM EGGS

BREADCRUMBS AS NEEDED

VEGETABLE OIL FOR FRYING

CINNAMON SUGAR (page 181) TO SERVE

APPLE SAUCE (page 181) TO SERVE

Oma's Waffeln
Grandma's Waffles

Waffles were always a treat, and often we would have them on Saturday evenings. Supper on Saturdays used to be quite early, because we had to catch Star Trek *on TV, which was on at 6.10pm! We sat around the table, the electric waffle maker in the middle, and the waffles were eaten as soon as they were ready.*

Sift the flour and baking powder into a bowl and set aside.

Put the butter, salt and sugar into a big bowl. Using a hand mixer or the balloon whisk on a stand mixer, whisk together until it turns fluffy and changes colour. Whisk the egg yolks and vanilla bean paste into the butter mix. Add the milk, flour mixture and sparkling water bit by bit, alternating between the three.

Whisk the egg whites to soft peaks. Fold the egg whites into the batter.

This waffle batter is best used immediately. The cooking time depends on the waffle maker used, but the waffles should be a bit crisp and a light golden colour when ready.

Serve with icing sugar, cinnamon sugar or apple sauce.

makes about 12, depending on the size of your waffle maker

330G PLAIN FLOUR

½ TEASPOON BAKING POWDER

150G UNSALTED BUTTER, CUBED, ROOM TEMPERATURE

1 PINCH SALT

100G CASTER SUGAR

4 MEDIUM EGGS, SEPARATED

1 TEASPOON VANILLA BEAN PASTE

330ML WHOLE MILK, ROOM TEMPERATURE

160ML SPARKLING WATER

FOR TOPPING
ICING SUGAR, CINNAMON SUGAR (page 181)
OR APPLE SAUCE (page 181)

Dampfnudeln
Sweet Dumplings
Steamed in Milk

You need a deep frying pan or a saucepan of 20cm diameter with a tight-fitting lid for these. If your lid has venting holes or lets out steam, it is important to cover those areas with a damp tea towel.

*makes 4
(in a 20cm pan)*

60G UNSALTED BUTTER,
ROOM TEMPERATURE

125ML WHOLE MILK,
PLUS EXTRA FOR COOKING

250G BREAD FLOUR

40G CASTER SUGAR,
PLUS EXTRA FOR SPRINKLING

1 PINCH SALT

1 TEASPOON INSTANT YEAST

1 MEDIUM EGG

Combine 35g of the butter and the milk in a saucepan or bowl, and heat on the stove or in the microwave until lukewarm.

Combine the flour, 20g of the sugar, the salt and yeast in a bowl. Pour in the milk and butter, add the egg and knead using your hands or a stand mixer fitted with a dough hook until a smooth ball forms. Cover and leave to prove in a warm place until well risen (use the poke test on page 201 to check if it's ready). Divide the dough into four equal pieces and shape them into balls. Cover them with a plastic bag or a tea towel and leave to prove for 30 minutes.

Meanwhile, add enough milk to cover the bottom of your pan or saucepan to a 1cm depth, plus the remaining butter and sugar.

When the dumplings have risen, bring the milk mixture to the boil, then reduce the heat so that it simmers. Pour a little bit of sugar into a bowl, dip the bottom of each dumpling into the sugar and place the dumpling in the milk. Once all dumplings are in the pan, put on the lid and seal it if necessary. Steam the dumplings for about 30 minutes. You must not open the lid, or the dumplings will shrink and become unpalatable. It is hard to judge when they are done – you will have to listen. At first you hear the water boiling. This will go on for most of the time. When the noise changes to more of a crackling sound, like frying, the water has evaporated, and the dumplings are done. Continue to fry for another minute or two. You should also notice a light caramel scent.

There is no way to judge this by eye, even with a glass lid. And it is normal to have a few mishaps before mastering the recipe. But it is incredibly rewarding to make and delicious to eat. Dampfnudeln are best served with vanilla custard or Weinschaum-Crème (page 187). Fruit compote and vanilla ice cream are also great companions.

Salzige Dampfnudeln
Dumplings
Steamed in Salt Water

This recipe is simpler than the dumplings steamed in milk (opposite), and it is probably more widespread in Germany. Using less sugar, and a brine for steaming means that these dumplings are equally suited to accompany a savoury meal like goulash, or as a dessert with custard or wine sauce.

Combine the butter and milk in a saucepan or bowl, and heat on the hob or in the microwave until lukewarm. The butter needs to be lukewarm as well.

Put the flour, salt and yeast into a bowl and mix. Add the milk mixture and knead using your hands or a stand mixer fitted with a dough hook until a smooth ball forms.

Cover the dough and leave it to prove in a warm place for about 1 hour until well risen. You can use the poke test (see page 201) to check if it's ready. Divide the dough into four equal pieces and shape them into balls. Cover them with a plastic bag or a tea towel and let them prove for about 30 minutes.

Meanwhile add water to a 20cm diameter pan to a 1cm depth and add the oil and ½ teaspoon of salt. Bring the water and oil to the boil and turn down the heat so that it simmers. Transfer the dumplings to the pan with enough space to expand and cover with the lid. (This recipe needs a tightly-fitting lid.) Steam the dumplings for about 30 minutes. You must not open the lid, or the dumplings will shrink and become unpalatable. It is hard to judge when they are done – you will have to listen. At first you hear the water boiling. This will go on for most of the time. When the noise changes to more of a crackling sound, like frying, the water has evaporated and the dumplings are done. Continue to fry for another minute or two.

Serve hot with savoury dishes, or with custard or fruit compote.

*makes 4
(in a 20cm pan)*

15G UNSALTED BUTTER,
ROOM TEMPERATURE

150ML WHOLE MILK, LUKEWARM

250G BREAD FLOUR

5G SALT, PLUS ½ TEASPOON FOR STEAMING

3G INSTANT YEAST

1 TABLESPOON VEGETABLE OIL

EARLY ON I WAS FASCINATED BY MOTORS AND GEARS, AND I HAD
TO SEE WHAT WAS GOING ON UNDER THE COVERS. THIS FASCINATION IS VERY
PROMINENT IN MY APPROACH TO BAKING AS WELL.

Traybakes

There is no easier way to make cake for a large number of people than a traybake. They can be easily portioned in squares, and everybody gets pretty much the same amount of filling. In Germany traybakes are very popular at church bazaars, village fêtes, birthday parties and the like, but you can also buy them at bakery outlets.

There is a huge number of recipes for traybakes, and one specific kind of traybake deserves a special mention: Streuselkuchen, or 'crumble cake'. The main difference between English crumble and German Streusel is the texture. English crumble is akin to breadcrumbs, whereas Streusel is chunkier. The Streusel dough is also worked just that little bit longer, which means it holds together more. The resulting texture and flavour are surprisingly different.

Often, Streuselkuchen has a yeasted base, but it can also be made with a shortbread-like pastry, or a sponge. There are no limits when it comes to fillings – fruit or custard in any combination are all possible – plus finely ground nuts or cocoa can be added to the Streusel too.

If being cooked as a traybake, Streuselkuchen will have a yeasted base or a sponge base, and can be found almost everywhere in Germany, from street corner bakeries to posh cafés to village festivals. In its simplest form it is just a yeasted base topped with Streusel – something I ate a lot of during my time at university!

In this chapter I have included options to use a yeasted base or a sponge base, but please feel free to experiment.

Einfacher Streuselkuchen
Simple Streusel Cake

This cake is the easiest Streuselkuchen to make, as it requires no filling, and it is surprisingly satisfying. When taking a bite, you immediately experience the contrast between the crunchy, sweet Streusel topping and the soft, flaky base. A simple but divine match. It was one of my favourite takeaway treats when strolling through the streets of Freiburg.

makes 20 slices

1 PORTION STREUSEL (page 192)

1 PORTION BASIC YEASTED SWEET DOUGH (page 194) OR RICH YEASTED SWEET DOUGH (page 195)

UNSALTED BUTTER FOR GREASING

Prepare the Streusel as directed on page 192.

Prepare the yeasted base according to the recipe on page 194 or 195. After the first prove, roll it out to fit a 35 x 28cm baking tray.

Lightly butter the baking tray and line it with the dough. Leave to rise at room temperature for 30 minutes. This is to allow the dough to relax into its shape in the baking tray.

Meanwhile, preheat the oven to 170°C fan/gas mark 5.

Using a brush or spray bottle, moisten the surface of the yeasted base. Water from the tap is fine.

Sprinkle the Streusel onto the yeasted base, making sure it is evenly distributed, then bake for about 30 minutes until the Streusel is light golden brown – the edges will be a bit darker.

Leave to cool in the tray for 5 minutes, then remove the cake from the tray and place on a wire rack to cool completely. This is best eaten fresh, but can be frozen or kept in an airtight container for up to 3 days.

Streuselkuchen mit Obst
Crumble Cake
with apples, rhubarb
or summer fruit

This cake combines custard (or in German: Pudding) and fruit so is essentially a crumble that you can eat with your hands.

Prepare the Streusel as directed on page 192. Prepare the vanilla pudding as directed on page 185.

If using a yeasted base, prepare the yeasted base as directed on page 194 or 195. After the first prove, roll it out to fit a 35 x 28cm baking tray.

Lightly butter the baking tray and line it with the dough. Leave to rise at room temperature for 30 minutes. This is to allow the dough to relax into its shape in the baking tray. If using a basic sponge, spread the batter evenly in the baking tray.

Meanwhile, preheat the oven to 170°C fan/gas mark 5.

Place all the fruit in a bowl and mix with the sugar.

Once the base is ready, spread the base with a layer of vanilla pudding, followed by a layer of the fruit, distributing it evenly. Lightly press the fruit into the pudding, then sprinkle the Streusel on top, making sure that it, too, is evenly distributed.

If using a yeasted base, bake for about 30 minutes until the Streusel is light golden brown – the edge of the yeasted base will be a bit darker. If using the basic sponge base, bake for about 50 minutes.

Leave to cool in the tray for 5 minutes, then remove the cake from the tray and place on a wire rack to cool completely. This is best eaten fresh, but can be frozen or kept in an airtight container for up to 3 days.

makes 20 slices

1 PORTION STREUSEL (page 192)

1 PORTION VANILLA PUDDING WITH EGG
(page 185)

1 PORTION OF BASIC YEASTED SWEET DOUGH
(page 194) OR RICH YEASTED SWEET
DOUGH (page 195) OR BASIC SPONGE (page 192)

UNSALTED BUTTER FOR GREASING

2 APPLES, PEELED, CORED AND CUBED
(use apples that stay firm when cooked,
e.g. Granny Smith)

300G RHUBARB, TRIMMED AND CUT INTO 1CM
PIECES, OR SUMMER FRUIT (frozen)

30G CASTER SUGAR

makes 25 slices

FOR THE CAKE
350G UNSALTED BUTTER,
ROOM TEMPERATURE

270G CASTER SUGAR

7 MEDIUM EGGS,
ROOM TEMPERATURE

450G PLAIN FLOUR

15G BAKING POWDER

50G COCOA POWDER

2 X 400G JARS MORELLO CHERRIES
IN SYRUP
(or similar, pitted cherries)

FOR THE BUTTERCREAM
1 PORTION VANILLA PUDDING
(page 184)

250G UNSALTED BUTTER, CUBED,
ROOM TEMPERATURE

80G ICING SUGAR

FOR THE GLAZE
350G DARK CHOCOLATE
(70% cocoa solids), BROKEN INTO PIECES

25G COCONUT OIL
OR UNSALTED BUTTER

Donauwellen
(The Waves of the Danube)

This cake is a real classic. The source of the Danube is in the Black Forest, so it is no surprise that the flavours are very similar to Black Forest gateau. But Donauwellen looks very different, and no alcohol is involved. When the cake is assembled you just see a flat piece of chocolate from above. Cut into it and the waves are revealed: during baking the cherries sink into the layers of chocolate sponge and plain sponge beneath to create the wave pattern. The cake is topped with a vanilla buttercream and glazed with chocolate. The amounts given are for a large, deep baking tray.

Preheat the oven to 175°C/gas mark 6.

To prepare the batter, make sure the ingredients are at room temperature. If the eggs and butter are too cold the mix might split when combined.

Put the butter and 220g of the sugar in a bowl and whisk, using a hand mixer or a stand mixer fitted with the balloon whisk, until frothy and light. Add the eggs one by one while continuing to whisk, waiting for each egg to be incorporated well before adding the next.

Sift the flour and baking powder together. Mix this into the butter and eggs bit by bit.

Line a large, deep baking tray, approximately 30 x 40cm and 3cm deep with baking paper and spread half of the batter evenly onto it. For the chocolate batter, mix together the cocoa powder and remaining 50g sugar and sift it into the bowl with the plain batter. Mix well until the batter is smooth. Spread the chocolate batter evenly on top of the plain batter, trying not to disturb the plain batter underneath.

Place the cherries on top of the chocolate batter, about 3cm from each other, and very slightly push them into the batter.

Bake in the middle of the oven for about 25 minutes; a skewer inserted into the centre of the cake should come out clean. Leave to cool in the tray.

For the buttercream, prepare the vanilla pudding as directed on page 184. Whisk the butter with the icing sugar until it is very frothy and light. While the vanilla pudding is still lukewarm, whisk it into the butter bit by bit.

Once the cake is cool, spread the buttercream evenly on top.

For the chocolate glaze, put the chocolate into a heatproof bowl together with the oil and melt over a bain-marie, or in a microwave. Be careful not to overheat the chocolate. Once it is melted, let it cool down to about 30°C, stirring gently without incorporating any air. Spread the chocolate glaze evenly on top of the buttercream.

Put the cake in a cool place and let the chocolate glaze set.

Trim the edges and cut into portion-sized rectangles to serve. This cake keeps for at least 3 days in an airtight container, longer in the fridge.

Butterkuchen
Butter Cake

This cake is very popular because it's so easy to make, plus it's an ideal way to show off your fluffy yeasted base.

makes 20 slices

1 PORTION BASIC YEASTED SWEET DOUGH
OR RICH YEASTED SWEET DOUGH
(page 194 or page 195)

150G UNSALTED BUTTER, COLD, CUBED,
PLUS EXTRA FOR GREASING

150G CASTER SUGAR

100G FLAKED ALMONDS

Line a 35 x 28cm baking tray with baking paper.

Prepare the yeasted base as directed on page 194 or 195. After the first prove, roll it out to fit the prepared baking tray.

Lightly butter the baking tray and line it with the dough. Leave to rise at room temperature for 30 minutes. This is to allow the dough to relax into its shape in the baking tray.

Push the butter cubes into the dough, about one every 4cm, and sprinkle with the sugar and almonds. Allow to rise for a further 15 minutes.

Meanwhile, preheat the oven to 170°C fan/gas mark 5.

Bake for 25–30 minutes until your cake has a beautiful golden colour. Take care not to burn the almonds. Watch the oven temperature, as many ovens are hotter than the dial setting. If the yeast base needs more time, cover the cake with foil and continue baking, checking every 5 minutes.

This cake can be eaten slightly warm. It is best eaten fresh, but can be kept for a couple of days in an airtight container, or portions can be frozen.

Pudding Streuselkuchen
Custard Crumble Cake

Custard (or in German: Pudding) is another very popular choice for a Streuselkuchen filling, and it is my personal favourite. The thickness of the custard layer may vary according to the taste of the baker. My choice would be to have enough pudding so that it shows up as a distinct layer rather than a thin spread, but anything is possible and tasty.

makes 20 slices

1 PORTION STREUSEL
(page 192)

1 PORTION VANILLA PUDDING WITH EGG
(page 185)

1 PORTION OF BASIC YEASTED SWEET DOUGH
(page 194) OR RICH YEASTED SWEET DOUGH
(page 195) OR BASIC SPONGE BASE (page 192)

UNSALTED BUTTER FOR GREASING

Prepare the Streusel as directed on page 192.

Prepare the vanilla pudding as directed on page 185.

Prepare the yeasted base as directed on page 194 or 195. After the first prove, roll it out to fit a 35 x 28cm baking tray.

Lightly butter the baking tray and line it with the dough. Leave to rise at room temperature for 30 minutes. This is to allow the dough to relax into its shape in the baking tray.

If using a basic sponge, spread the batter evenly in the baking tray.

Meanwhile, preheat the oven to 170°C fan/gas mark 5.

Once the base is ready, spread the pudding evenly over the top. The thickness of the pudding layer is down to personal taste, but the amounts given work well for me. Sprinkle the Streusel on top, making sure it's distributed evenly.

If using a yeasted base, bake for about 30 minutes until the Streusel is light golden brown – the edge of the yeasted base will be a bit darker. If using the basic sponge base, bake for about 50 minutes.

Leave to cool in the tray for 5 minutes, then remove the cake from the tray and place on a wire rack to cool completely. This is best eaten fresh, but can be frozen or kept in an airtight container for up to 3 days.

Apfel-Streuselkuchen
Apple Crumble Cake

Just adding apple cubes to a simple Streuselkuchen creates a very different cake. The apples introduce moistness, acidity and a third texture, creating a slice of cake that can be quite refreshing on a warm July day at a village fête.

Prepare the Streusel as directed on page 192.

If using a yeasted base, prepare the yeasted base according to the recipe on page 194 or 195. After the first prove, roll it out to fit a 35 x 28cm baking tray.

Lightly butter the baking tray and line it with the dough. Leave to rise at room temperature for 30 minutes. This is to allow the dough to relax into its shape in the baking tray.

If using a basic sponge, spread the batter evenly in the baking tray.

Meanwhile, preheat the oven to 170°C fan/gas mark 5.

Place the apples in a bowl, add the sugar and spices and mix well. Once the dough is ready, distribute the apples evenly over the surface and lightly press them down. Sprinkle the Streusel on top, making sure it's distributed evenly.

If using a yeasted base, bake for about 30 minutes until the Streusel is light golden brown – the edge of the yeasted base will be a bit darker. If using the basic sponge base, bake for about 50 minutes.

Leave to cool in the tray for 5 minutes, then remove the cake from the tray and place on a wire rack to cool completely. This is best eaten fresh, but can be frozen or kept in an airtight container for up to 3 days.

makes 20 slices

1 PORTION STREUSEL (page 192)

1 PORTION OF BASIC YEASTED SWEET DOUGH (page 194) OR RICH YEASTED SWEET DOUGH (page 195) OR BASIC SPONGE BASE (page 192)

UNSALTED BUTTER FOR GREASING

5 FIRM, SLIGHTLY TART APPLES, PEELED, CORED AND CUBED

30G CASTER SUGAR

1 TEASPOON GROUND CINNAMON

½ TEASPOON GROUND CORIANDER

Schoko-Streuselkuchen mit Birne
Chocolate Pear Crumble Cake

A variation on the Birne Helene (pear Helene) theme. A teaspoon of ground cardamom is added to the base, and 25g of the flour in the Streusel is replaced with cocoa powder.

makes 20 slices

1 PORTION STREUSEL (page 192),
BUT SUBSTITUTE 25G FLOUR
WITH 25G COCOA POWDER

1 PORTION OF BASIC YEASTED SWEET DOUGH
(page 194) OR RICH YEASTED SWEET DOUGH
(page 195) OR BASIC SPONGE BASE (page 192)
WITH 1 TEASPOON GROUND CARDAMOM
ADDED TO THE FLOUR

UNSALTED BUTTER FOR GREASING

4 FIRM PEARS, SUCH AS CONFERENCE,
PEELED, CORED AND CUBED

30G CASTER SUGAR

Prepare the Streusel as directed on page 192, substituting 25g of the flour with 25g cocoa powder.

If using a yeasted base, prepare the yeasted base as directed on page 194 or 195, adding the cardamom to the flour. After the first prove, roll it out to fit a 35 x 28cm baking tray.

Lightly butter the baking tray and line it with the dough. Leave to rise at room temperature for 30 minutes. This is to allow the dough to relax into its shape in the baking tray.

If using a basic sponge, spread the batter evenly in the baking tray.

Meanwhile, preheat the oven to 170°C fan/gas mark 5.

Place the pears in a bowl and mix with the sugar.

Once the base is ready, spread evenly with the pieces of pear, lightly pressing them into the dough, then sprinkle the Streusel on top, making sure it, too, is evenly distributed.

If using a yeasted base, bake for about 30 minutes until the edge of the yeasted base is a medium golden brown. If using the basic sponge base, bake for about 50 minutes.

Leave to cool in the tray for 5 minutes, then remove the cake from the tray and place on a wire rack to cool completely. This is best eaten fresh, but can be frozen or kept in an airtight container for up to 3 days.

Schoko-Apfel-Streuselkuchen
Chocolate Apple Crumble Cake

This Streuselkuchen variation is for the chocolate addicts. The soft, moist, acidic apple pieces and the sweet, rich chocolate custard are a great match, sandwiched between crisp Streusel and a flaky base, every bite is a an adventure. This cake is my family's favourite Streuselkuchen.

makes 20 slices

1 PORTION BASIC YEASTED SWEET DOUGH
(page 194) OR RICH YEASTED SWEET
DOUGH (page 195) OR BASIC SPONGE
BASE (page 192)

1 PORTION STREUSEL
(page 192)

1 PORTION VANILLA PUDDING WITH EGG
(page 185)

100G DARK CHOCOLATE
(70% cocoa solids), BROKEN INTO PIECES

UNSALTED BUTTER FOR GREASING

5 FIRM, SLIGHTLY TART APPLES, SUCH AS
GRANNY SMITH, PEELED, CORED AND CUBED

30G CASTER SUGAR

½ TEASPOON GROUND CLOVES

Prepare the yeasted base as directed on page 194 or 195. Prepare the Streusel as directed on page 192. Prepare the vanilla pudding as directed on page 185 and allow to cool. Melt the chocolate either in a microwave or in a bowl set over a pan of simmering water (but don't allow the bowl to touch the water). Make sure the chocolate is just liquid; overheating will break the chocolate and render it unusable.

Once the custard has cooled, stir in the melted chocolate.

If using a yeasted base, after the base has had its first prove, roll it out to fit a 35 x 28cm baking tray.

Lightly butter the baking tray and line it with the dough. Leave to rise at room temperature for 30 minutes. This is to allow the dough to relax into its shape in the baking tray. If using a basic sponge, spread the batter evenly in the baking tray.

Meanwhile, preheat the oven to 170°C fan/gas mark 5. Place the apples in a bowl, add the sugar and ground cloves and mix well.

Spread a layer of the chocolate pudding evenly over the base. Distribute the apples evenly over the top, lightly push them down into the custard, then sprinkle with the Streusel, making sure that it, too, is evenly distributed.

If using a yeasted base, bake for about 30 minutes until the Streusel is light golden brown, the edge of the yeasted base will be a bit darker. If using the basic sponge base, bake for about 50 minutes.

Leave to cool in the tray for 5 minutes, then remove from the tray and place on a wire rack to cool completely. This is best eaten fresh, but can be frozen or kept in an airtight container for up to 3 days

THE HOUSE WHERE I GREW UP. THIS PHOTO IS FROM AROUND 1950.

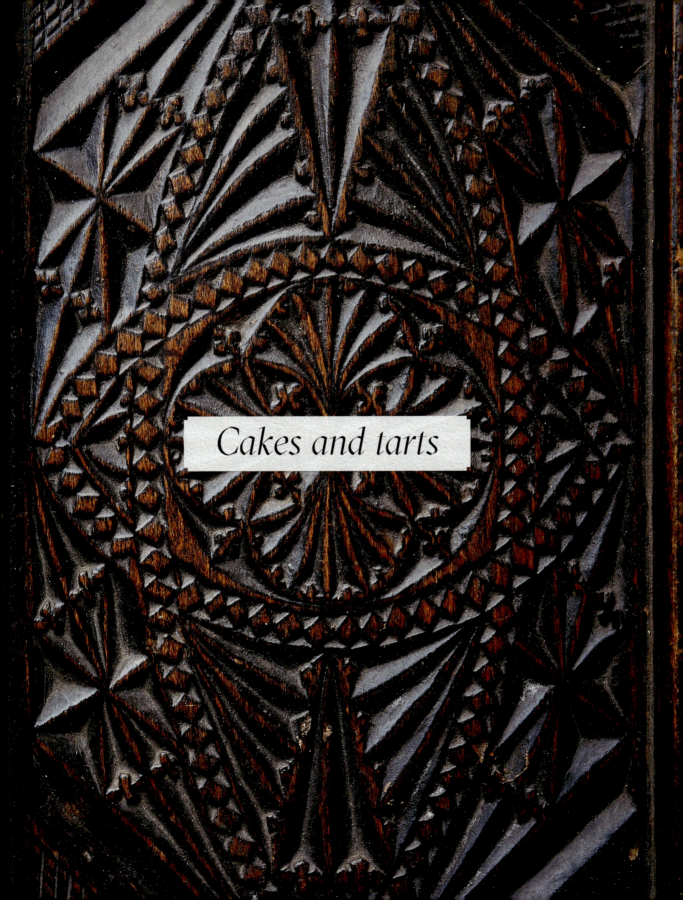

Cakes and tarts

The village I grew up in is on the outskirts of Freiburg. Perched in a long valley, even nowadays it still feels remote from the city. On the many occasions when we went into town by public transport, we had to walk a little way to catch the bus, then change on to the tram, which eventually would arrive right in the centre of Freiburg. During the journey the scenery outside changed. Starting out with views of forest, meadows and cows, as the journey progressed, the houses got bigger and less familiar, and I knew we would arrive soon when the tram crossed the river Dreisam and then passed through an old gate with murals of St George.

This change of scenery, and the smells, sounds and unfamiliar movements of bus and tram was a great prelude for the two things I always looked forward to most: the toy shops and the cake buffet in the department stores. Those department stores changed a lot over time, and the victims of the change in the 80s were the huge cafés on their top floors, whose space was repurposed for selling camping equipment.

The views of the cathedral and market square from those rooftop cafés were stunning. The furniture was wooden, solid and durable, and a fleet of waitresses served the huge crowd that regularly gathered every afternoon to have their coffee and cake. The cake buffet was gigantic, in my memory. I had my favourite cake – the Black Forest gateau – but I was always attracted to the very neat mousse cakes and Charlottes.

The store's bakers seemed to have an endless repertoire of interior and exterior cake designs.

It is very fitting that my son Benjamin's choice of birthday cake from early on was a fruit Charlotte; he asked for one for his eighth birthday, and this wish led to a great boost for my baking!

In terms of tarts, Linzer Torte has a very special place in our family. My mother used to make it all year round, with the help of my brother and me. But for Advent and Christmas we always made several Linzer tarts at a time to store them, as they improve a lot over time. They were then a coffee table staple on Christmas Day and Boxing Day, when relatives came round for a visit.

For our wedding, Sophia and I asked my mother to make Linzer Torte as a treat after the ceremony, which she happily did. All our guests had walked a long way through wind and rain to the cliffs of the Seven Sisters. During the service the clouds broke, and we were blessed with sunshine in that most beautiful scenery. After the ceremony, we served my mother's Linzer Torte, which she brought all the way from Germany, along with special wine from Freiburg. Then we headed off to the top of the cliffs, to have a dance while the Klezmer band played.

All the following cakes would not have been out of place in one of the department store cafés of my childhood.

Schwarzwälder Kirschtorte
Black Forest Gateau

serves 12

FOR THE CHERRY FILLING
450G MORELLO CHERRIES
OR BLACK CHERRIES IN SYRUP (drained), PITTED

60ML KIRSCH

250ML SYRUP FROM CHERRIES

40G CORNFLOUR

2 TABLESPOONS WATER

120G CASTER SUGAR

FOR THE KIRSCH SYRUP
60ML WATER

60G CASTER SUGAR

60ML KIRSCH

FOR THE SHORTCRUST PASTRY
100G PLAIN FLOUR, PLUS EXTRA FOR DUSTING

30G CASTER SUGAR

80G UNSALTED BUTTER, CUBED

1 TABLESPOON BEATEN EGG

½ TEASPOON VANILLA BEAN PASTE

APRICOT JAM, TO COVER SHORTCRUST BOTTOM

As every viewer of The Great British Bake Off *knows, this is my personal favourite. It is the measure by which I would judge a café or a bakery. The balance between cream, kirsch and chocolate needs to be just right. Shortcuts don't work, and I would be very reluctant to change this flavour profile into something novel. Not every pâtissier adds a shortcrust bottom, but I find that a little crunch makes an otherwise very soft texture far more interesting. Morello cherries are preferred, but black cherries in light syrup are OK, although not so flavourful.*

Don't be intimidated by the long list of ingredients and steps — each single step is quite easy, and the outcome will be rewarding, I promise. Many of the components can be prepared the day before the cake is needed: shortcrust bottom, sponges, cherry filling and kirsch syrup. With those things in place, assembly is very quick.

For the cherry filling, soak the drained cherries in the kirsch overnight. Drain the cherries and reserve the kirsch. Put the kirsch into a measuring jug and add enough of the reserved syrup to get 300ml of liquid.

Dissolve the cornflour in the water and add to the kirsch mixture in a saucepan. Add the sugar and carefully bring to the boil while stirring. Once the liquid has boiled and thickened, and no longer tastes of starch, take it off the heat and carefully stir in the cherries. Set aside and leave to cool completely.

For the kirsch syrup, combine the water and sugar in a small saucepan and bring to the boil while stirring. Once the sugar has dissolved completely, take it off the heat and leave to cool completely. Add the kirsch.

To make the shortcrust pastry, put all the ingredients in a bowl and mix with your hands until the dough is smooth. Wrap in clingfilm and set aside in the fridge for about 30 minutes until the dough is just firm enough to roll out.

Preheat the oven to 180°C fan/gas mark 6. Lightly grease a 25cm springform or sandwich tin.
continued overleaf

FOR THE CHOCOLATE SPONGE
6 MEDIUM EGGS

160G CASTER SUGAR

2G SALT

90G PLAIN FLOUR

55G CORNFLOUR

30G COCOA POWDER

50G UNSALTED BUTTER,
MELTED, PLUS EXTRA FOR GREASING

FOR THE CREAM FILLING
500ML DOUBLE CREAM

30ML KIRSCH

40G ICING SUGAR, SIFTED

TO FINISH
300ML DOUBLE CREAM

10G ICING SUGAR, SIFTED

6 GLACÉ CHERRIES, HALVED

CHOCOLATE SHAVINGS AS NEEDED

On a floured surface, roll out the dough to a circle about 3mm thick. Transfer the dough to the prepared tin, cutting off any surplus as only the bottom of the tin needs to be covered. Prick the pastry bottom with a fork so that trapped air can escape during baking.

Bake for 8–10 minutes until the edges start to brown.

For the chocolate sponge, lightly grease a 25cm springform cake tin and line the bottom with baking paper. Increase the oven temperature to 200°C fan/gas mark 7.

Sift the flour, cornflour and cocoa powder together into a bowl. Set aside.

Put some water in a saucepan and bring to the boil. This is for heating the bowl with the eggs.

Put the eggs, sugar and salt in a bowl.

Place the bowl with the eggs over the simmering water and whisk with a hand mixer on medium speed until the eggs reach a temperature of about 43°C. The bowl should not touch the water in the saucepan beneath.

Take the bowl off the boiling water and continue whisking on high speed until the eggs are cold and have reached the ribbon stage, i.e. when the whisk is pulled out of the mix and moved across the surface it creates a ribbon of egg froth that slowly disappears.

Fold the sifted flour mixture into the eggs, then stir the melted butter in to the mixture.

Pour the batter into the prepared tin and bake for about 15 minutes until a skewer inserted into the centre comes out clean. Leave to cool before taking out of the tin.

Cut the top off the cooled sponge to even it out, if necessary. Cut the sponge into three equal layers, reserving the most even layer for the top.

For the cream filling, combine the double cream, kirsch and icing sugar and whip to stiff peaks.

Place the shortcrust bottom on a cake board. Heat some apricot jam so that it is just liquid enough to be spread easily. Cover the shortcrust bottom with a thin layer of apricot jam.

Place the bottom sponge layer on top of the shortcrust bottom and brush with kirsch syrup.

Transfer some of the cream filling into a piping bag with a large round nozzle and pipe two concentric rings, starting at the edge, and a bullseye. Fill the gaps with cherry filling. It should be thick enough to hold its place. This should look like a target disc or dartboard with five zones, from the middle: cream – cherries – cream – cherries – cream.

Select your second sponge, turn it upside down and brush the underside with kirsch syrup. Place the sponge brushed-side down on top of the bottom sponge and filling.

Repeat the steps – brush the top of the sponge – apply cream and cherry filling – brush the bottom of third sponge and place it on top of the cake, syrup-side down. Gently press down the top sponge and even out any irregularities. If there is a bit of cream filling left, use it to apply a thin crumb layer.

To finish off the cake, whip the cream and icing sugar to soft peaks. Don't over-whip or it will set and break when piping. The starch in the icing sugar will stabilize the whipped cream and help it keep its shape for longer.

Reserve enough of the whipped cream in a piping bag with a medium star nozzle to pipe 12 pirouettes (the classic decoration) and any other decorations you fancy. Cover the cake evenly with the remaining cream and smooth the surface. Pipe 12 pirouettes, one for each slice of cake, around the edge. Top each pirouette with half a glacé cherry. Cover the sides and the centre of the cake with chocolate shavings.

This cake will be good for 3 days. It needs to be kept in the fridge.

FOR THE FILLING
200ML WHOLE MILK

450ML DOUBLE CREAM

1 VANILLA POD

5 MEDIUM EGG YOLKS

60G CASTER SUGAR

35G CORNFLOUR

2 GELATINE LEAVES

ZEST OF 1 LEMON

2 TEASPOONS VANILLA BEAN PASTE

FOR THE YEASTED BASE
340G BREAD FLOUR

40G CASTER SUGAR

5G INSTANT YEAST

2G SALT

170ML WHOLE MILK, LUKEWARM

20G UNSALTED BUTTER, ROOM TEMPERATURE,
PLUS EXTRA FOR GREASING

1 MEDIUM EGG YOLK

ZEST OF 1 LEMON

FOR THE TOPPING
80G UNSALTED BUTTER

80G CASTER SUGAR

80G FLAKED ALMONDS

50ML DOUBLE CREAM

30G HONEY

Bienenstich
Bee-Sting Cake

Bienenstich is my mother's favourite, and an absolute classic. But the way it presents itself in cafés can be quite varied. The common elements are: a yeasted cake, topped with an almond sugar mix, sliced into two layers, and filled with some sort of cream. No matter how it has been made, the huge difference in textures make it the messiest German cake to eat, but that is part of the fun!

The filling can be made the day before if you like. Pour the milk and 300ml of the double cream into a saucepan. Split the vanilla pod and scrape out the seeds. Add the seeds to the milk and bring to scalding point. While the milk is heating up, place the egg yolks, sugar and cornflour in a bowl and whisk until smooth.

Once the milk is hot, slowly pour one third of it into the egg yolks while stirring. Pour this mixture back into the saucepan while stirring and return the saucepan to the heat. Slowly bring to the boil. When it starts boiling, quickly take the saucepan off the heat and pour the custard into a bowl. Take care not to overheat this custard: the starch prevents the egg yolk from coagulating, but the fat of the cream can separate from the mixture, which makes it unusable. Cover the surface with clingfilm to prevent a skin forming and set aside to cool.

To make the yeasted base, put all the ingredients in a bowl and, using your hands, mix and knead until a smooth ball forms. Continue kneading for another couple of minutes – a short knead is enough for this cake. Cover and leave to rest for 2 hours at room temperature.

Once the yeasted dough has proved, lightly grease a 25cm springform cake tin with butter.

Roll out the dough to a disc the size of the prepared tin – you don't need flour on the work surface – and transfer it into the tin. It should stretch all the way to the sides of the tin without creating a rim. Make sure you have an even thickness. Set aside.

To prepare the topping, put all the ingredients into a saucepan and heat over a medium heat, stirring constantly until the mixture thickens. This can take a few minutes. It should be spreadable but not runny, and not caramelized. Once this consistency is reached, let the mixture cool a bit while stirring.

With a teaspoon, place little heaps of the warm topping on top of the base in the tin. Make sure they are equally distributed. Now spread the topping to cover the base evenly, using a spatula or a pastry knife. This is an essential step: if the topping is uneven the cake will balloon at the thinner spots.

Let the cake rest for another 30 minutes. You don't need to cover it because of the topping.

Meanwhile, preheat the oven to 180°C/gas mark 4.
continued overleaf

Bake in the lower third of the oven for about 25 minutes. The colour should be a nice medium golden brown, like Florentines. Leave the cake to cool for 15 minutes, then carefully remove from the tin so you do not rip the topping apart. At this point you can use a knife to mark the slices and even cut carefully through the topping – it will make it much easier to serve the cake later. Transfer to a wire rack and let cool completely.

The assembly should be done as close to eating as possible. To finish the filling, soak the gelatine leaves in cold water. Add the lemon zest and vanilla bean paste to the custard and whisk until it is smooth. Whisk the remaining 150ml double cream until it is moderately stiff.

Take the gelatine leaves out of the water and put them in a small pan. Heat them until they melt – this will be very quick. Add the liquid gelatine to the custard and whisk. Fold in the whipped cream.

Cut the cake horizontally. Remove the top – don't turn it upside down. Spread the filling on the bottom of the Bienenstich; it should be at least as thick as the bottom cake layer. A piping bag with a big round nozzle is very useful for this. Place the top of the Bienenstich on top of the filling and lightly squeeze down.

Let the cream set a little while – ideally put the cake in the fridge for 20 minutes or so.

Bienenstich is best eaten fresh and needs to be kept cool.

serves 12

FOR THE SPONGES
6 MEDIUM EGGS, SEPARATED

175G CASTER SUGAR

90G PLAIN FLOUR

85G CORNFLOUR

60G UNSALTED BUTTER, MELTED

FOR THE FILLING
250G MARZIPAN
(page 189 or ready-made)

50ML WHISKEY

FOR THE GANACHE
150G CHOCOLATE (54% cocoa solids),
BROKEN INTO PIECES

200ML DOUBLE CREAM

Herren-Torte
Gentlemen's Cake

This cake with its many layers was one of the cakes that attracted me to those huge cake displays in department stores. There are several traditional cakes and desserts in Germany that contain the word Herren *in their name, the German word for 'gentlemen'. It is always a hint that strong, unusual flavours are being used. The original Herren-Torte was invented in the 1930s and features thin sponges alternating with wine-flavoured marzipan, but in my recipe I am using whiskey.*

For the sponges, prepare eight sheets of baking paper. Using a pencil, draw a circle of 25cm diameter on each of the sheets of paper. Turn the paper upside down so that the batter won't come into contact with the pencil.

Preheat the oven to 200°C fan/gas mark 7.

Divide the eggs whites and yolks between two big heatproof bowls. Pour half the sugar into the yolks. Beat the egg whites to soft peaks. Slowly add the remaining sugar bit by bit and whip to stiff peaks.

Sift the flour and cornflour together.

Over a pan of boiling water, whisk the sugar and egg yolks until they reach a temperature of about 43°C. Remove the bowl and continue whisking until the egg yolks are pale, frothy and creamy. Fold one third of the egg white into the egg yolks. Then fold in the remaining egg white. Fold in the flour mixture, followed by the melted butter.

The batter is enough for eight sponges. Depending on your equipment you can bake up to three sponges in one batch.

Spread the batter thinly inside the circles on the baking paper. Transfer the baking paper onto baking sheets and bake for 6–8 minutes. Don't overbake; the thin sponges can dry out very quickly and get brittle. Leave to cool and

repeat the previous steps until you have baked all eight sponges.

For the filling, knead the marzipan to soften it and break it into little pieces. Add the whiskey and stir until you have a smooth paste without any lumps.

To assemble the cake, make sure all eight sponges are the same size. Trim them if necessary. Place the bottom sponge on a cake tray and thinly cover with whiskey filling. Place the next sponge on top of the whiskey filling and coat thinly. Continue in this way until you have added all the sponges. Use whiskey filling to cover the sides and the top of the cake – only a very thin layer is necessary to even out little irregularities.

For the ganache, break the chocolate into little pieces and put them into a bowl. Pour the double cream into a pan and bring to scalding point. Pour the hot double cream over the chocolate and wait for about 2 minutes. Then stir the mixture using a whisk, but don't beat in any air bubbles.

Once the ganache is shiny, use it to coat the cake. Let the ganache set, then mark the cake slices with the back of a knife. For decoration, melt some chocolate and pipe the letter H (for Herren) on each slice. This cake improves in flavour over time and keeps very well in an airtight container for 3 days.

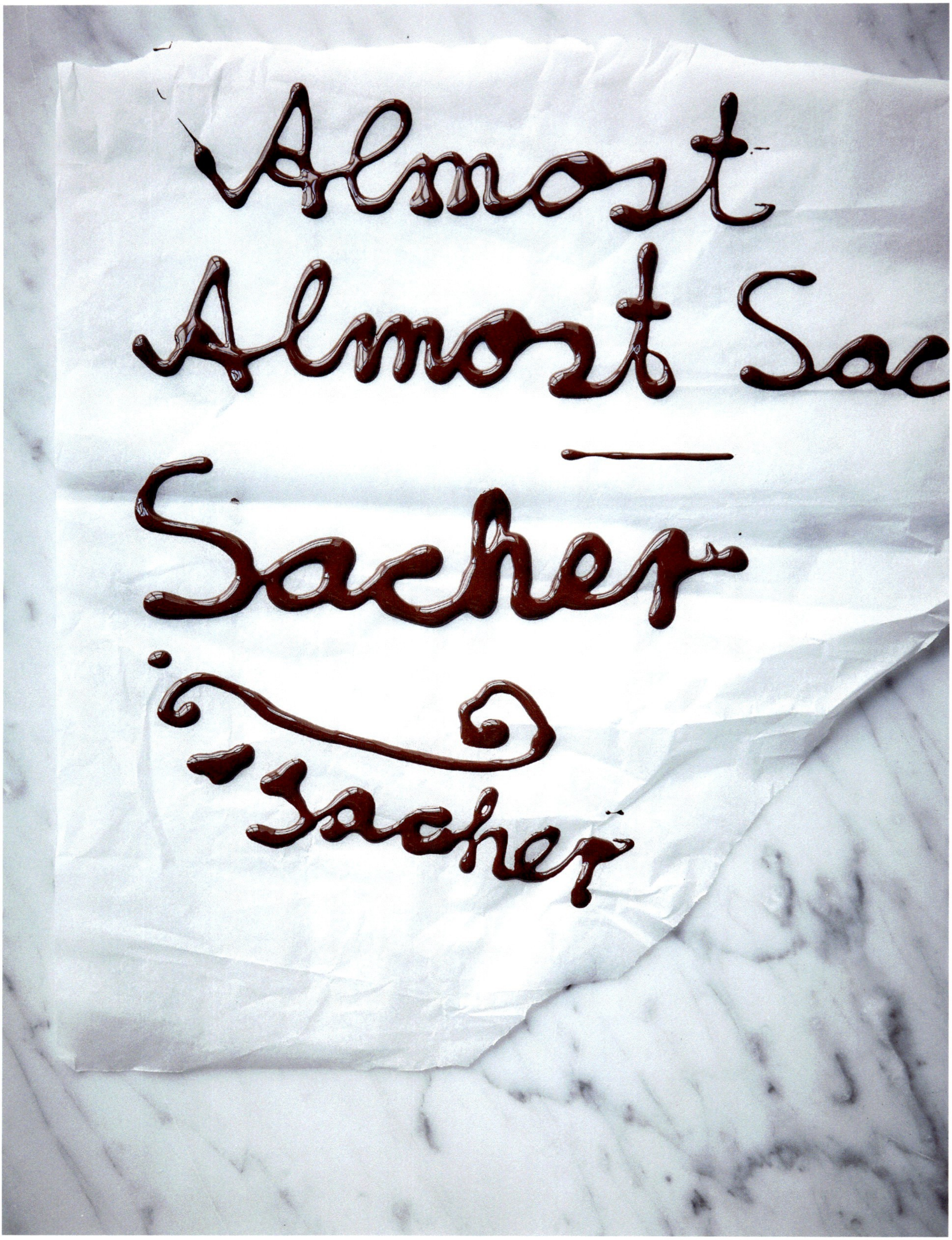

Almost Sacher Torte

serves 16

FOR THE SHORTCRUST PASTRY
100G PLAIN FLOUR, PLUS EXTRA FOR DUSTING

30G CASTER SUGAR

80G UNSALTED BUTTER,
CUBED, PLUS EXTRA FOR GREASING

1 TABLESPOON BEATEN EGG

FOR THE SACHER SPONGE
140G CHOCOLATE (70% cocoa solids),
BROKEN INTO PIECES

150G UNSALTED BUTTER, CUBED,
ROOM TEMPERATURE

50G ICING SUGAR

6 MEDIUM EGGS, SEPARATED

100G CASTER SUGAR

120G PLAIN FLOUR

20G COCOA POWDER

FOR THE GLAZE AND FILLING
400G ORANGE MARMALADE

50G UNSALTED BUTTER

200G DARK CHOCOLATE (70% cocoa solids)

180ML WATER

300G CASTER SUGAR

CHOCOLATE FOR PIPING, AS NEEDED

In the cake display of a German café, the Sacher Torte always stuck out for me. With its thick chocolate coating, dense sponges and minimalist filling, it had a promise of something different, and on occasion I would forgo my usual favourites and have a Sacher with a dollop of whipped cream. In its classic form the rich, dark chocolate flavour is perfectly balanced with sweet apricot jam.

Since coming to England I have really learned to appreciate orange marmalade, and for many years now I have been making my own Seville orange marmalade. Switching apricot for Seville orange introduces a light bitterness, creating a surprisingly different cake.

For the shortcrust pastry, put all the ingredients in a bowl and mix with your hands until the dough is smooth. Wrap in clingfilm and set aside in the fridge for about 30 minutes until the dough is just firm enough to roll out.

Preheat the oven to 180°C fan/gas mark 6. Lightly grease a 25cm springform cake tin or sandwich tin.

On a floured surface, roll out the dough to a circle about 3mm thick. Transfer the dough to the tin, cutting off any surplus as only the bottom needs to be covered. Prick the pastry bottom with a fork so that trapped air can escape during baking. Bake for 8–10 minutes until the edges start to brown.

For the Sacher sponge, melt the chocolate. Don't let it get too hot. You can set a plastic or metal bowl with the chocolate over a saucepan of water that has just boiled.

Line the bottom of a 25cm springform cake tin with baking paper and grease the sides. Reduce the oven temperature 165°C fan/gas mark 5.

Put the butter and icing sugar in a bowl and beat until frothy. Beat in the egg yolks one by one. Slowly whisk in the melted chocolate.

Whisk the egg whites to soft peaks, then gradually whisk in the sugar and continue to whisk until stiff peaks form and the egg whites are shiny. Sift the flour and cocoa powder together. Fold one third of the egg whites into the butter mixture. Then fold in the flour and cocoa powder. Finally, fold in the remaining egg whites.

Transfer the batter to the prepared tin, spread evenly and bake for 45 minutes until a skewer inserted into the centre comes out clean. Leave the sponge to cool in the tin for 30 minutes, then remove from the tin, peel off the baking paper and let cool completely.

Once cool, cut the sponge in half horizontally and trim the top, if necessary, to get an even sponge.

To assemble, lightly heat the marmalade so that it gets a bit runny. Add a bit of water if necessary. Place the shortcrust cake bottom on a cake board and thinly cover it with marmalade. Place the bottom sponge on top of the cake bottom and cover the sponge thinly with marmalade. (I've found that having a bit of peel in this layer adds a nice texture.) Put the remaining sponge on top. Strain the marmalade and cover the whole cake thinly with it.
To make the glaze, which is a classic chocolate icing called konserve-schokolade, put the butter and chocolate into a bowl – I like to use thin plastic or metal bowls because they transfer the heat quickly. Place the bowl over a saucepan with water that has just boiled. The bowl shouldn't touch the water.

Put the water and sugar into a saucepan and bring to the boil while stirring. Continue boiling the syrup, without stirring, until it reaches 108°C. Take the syrup off the heat and slowly add the chocolate mixture while stirring. Put the glaze back on to the heat and boil, stirring constantly, until the glaze reaches 104°C.

Take off the heat and gently stir while the glaze is cooling and thickening. The consistency should be such that some glaze poured over the back of a metal spoon sets about 4mm thick; the temperature of the glaze will be about 45°C.

Pour the glaze over the cake and spread it with a pastry knife so that the top and the sides of the cake are evenly covered. Leave the glaze to set.

To decorate, pipe chocolate ornaments, or the words 'Almost Sacher' on top.

This cake keeps extremely well and does not need cooling. The Sacher hotel sends their cakes worldwide, as they can keep for weeks in an airtight container.

Prinzregenten-Torte

This cake was created in honour of the Bavarian Prince Regent Luitpold in the nineteenth century. The layers symbolize the eight counties of Bavaria at the time. The build of this cake is very similar to the Herren-Torte on page 51, which was invented much later. This cake contains no alcohol, and the strongly contrasting layers make it a feast for the eyes as well as for the palate.

serves 12

FOR THE SPONGES
6 MEDIUM EGGS, SEPARATED

175G CASTER SUGAR

90G PLAIN FLOUR

85G CORNFLOUR

60G UNSALTED BUTTER, MELTED

FOR THE CHOCOLATE BUTTERCREAM
120G DARK CHOCOLATE (70% cocoa solids),
BROKEN INTO PIECES

250G UNSALTED BUTTER, ROOM TEMPERATURE

2 MEDIUM EGG YOLKS

150G ICING SUGAR

FOR THE GLAZE
200G CHOCOLATE (54% cocoa solids),
BROKEN INTO PIECES

50G UNSALTED BUTTER

For the sponges, prepare eight sheets of baking paper. Using a pencil, draw a circle of 25cm diameter on each of the sheets of paper. Turn the paper upside down so that the batter won't come into contact with the pencil.

Preheat the oven to 200°C fan/gas mark 7.

Divide the eggs whites and yolks between two big heatproof bowls. Pour half the sugar into the yolks. Beat the egg whites to soft peaks. Slowly add the remaining sugar bit by bit and whip to stiff peaks.

Sift the flour and cornflour together.

Over a pan of boiling water, whisk the sugar and egg yolks until they have a temperature of about 43°C. Remove the bowl and continue whisking until the egg yolks are pale, frothy and creamy. Fold one third of the egg white into the egg yolks. Then fold in the remaining egg white. Fold in the flour mixture, followed by the melted butter.

The batter is enough for eight sponges. Depending on your equipment you can bake up to three sponges in one batch.

Spread the batter thinly inside the circles on the baking paper. Transfer the baking paper onto baking sheets and bake for 6–8 minutes. Don't overbake; the thin sponges can dry out very quickly and get brittle.

Leave to cool and repeat the previous steps until you have baked all eight sponges.

For the chocolate buttercream, melt the chocolate in a heatproof bowl over a boiling water, making sure the bowl does not touch the water below (this is called a bain-marie). Once the chocolate has melted, set aside.

Whisk the butter until light and pale, then add egg yolks and icing sugar bit by bit while whisking. Continue whisking until the mixture is very light and frothy. Continue whisking while very slowly adding the liquid chocolate. Set aside.

To assemble the cake, make sure all eight sponges are the same size. Trim them if necessary.

Place the bottom sponge on a cake tray and thinly cover with chocolate buttercream. Place the next sponge on top of the buttercream and coat thinly. Continue in this way until you have used all the sponges. Use buttercream to cover the sides and the top of the cake; only a very thin layer is necessary to even out little irregularities. Put the cake in the fridge for at least 30 minutes.

Once the cake is cool and the buttercream is set, prepare the glaze. Melt the chocolate and butter over a bain-marie. Once melted, take the glaze off the heat and carefully stir the glaze while it is cooling. When it has the right consistency to cover the back of a spoon, apply the chocolate glaze to the cake, either using a brush, or by pouring. Leave the glaze to set.

Mark the cake slices lightly with the back of a knife. For decoration, pipe a pirouette of chocolate buttercream on to each slice. This cake improves in flavour over time and keeps very well in an airtight container for at least 3 days.

Mango-Maracuja Sahnetorte
Passion Fruit and Mango Charlotte Royale

I have always been attracted to the Charlotte royales they had in those big department store cake displays. Curiously I have never had one! But I've taken this opportunity to share my recipe for this stunning cake with its 1970s flair. The Genoese sponge forms the base of this cake, while the Joconde sponge creates the swirled pattern.

serves 16

FOR THE GENOESE SPONGE
4 MEDIUM EGGS

125G CASTER SUGAR

125G PLAIN FLOUR

25G UNSALTED BUTTER, MELTED

FOR THE JOCONDE SPONGE
100G GROUND ALMONDS

65G ICING SUGAR

35G PLAIN FLOUR

3 LARGE EGGS

1 LARGE EGG YOLK

3 LARGE EGG WHITES

35G CASTER SUGAR

35G UNSALTED BUTTER, MELTED

To make the Genoese sponge, line a 38 x 25cm baking tray with baking paper.

Preheat the oven to 180°C fan/gas mark 6.

Put the eggs and sugar in a heatproof bowl. Place over a pan of boiling water and whisk until the egg mix has reached 30°C or has doubled in volume. Take the egg mixture off the heat and whisk until the eggs are at room temperature – this takes about 10 minutes.

Fold in the flour, then fold in the melted butter. Transfer the batter to the prepared tray and carefully even out the batter. Bake for about 8–10 minutes. The sponge should begin to turn golden and spring back when gently touched. For cooling, remove the sponge with the baking paper from the tray and place it on a wire rack.

To make the Joconde sponge, line a baking sheet with baking paper. Increase the oven temperature to 200°C fan/gas mark 7.

In a large bowl, mix together the ground almonds, icing sugar and flour. Add the whole eggs and incorporate them. Add the egg yolk.

In a separate bowl, whisk the egg whites to soft peaks. Add the sugar and continue whisking the egg whites to stiff peaks. Fold one third of the egg whites into the flour and egg mixture, then fold in the remaining egg whites. Finally, fold in the melted butter.
continued overleaf

FOR THE CARAMEL FILLING
250G CASTER SUGAR

80ML WATER

150ML DOUBLE CREAM

75G UNSALTED BUTTER

FOR THE PASSION FRUIT
AND MANGO BAVARIAN CREAM
2 X 12G SACHETS GELATINE POWDER

4 TABLESPOONS WATER

9 PASSION FRUIT

1 MANGO, RIPE

160G CASTER SUGAR

600ML DOUBLE CREAM

FOR THE PASSION FRUIT GLAZE
1 SACHET (12G) GELATINE POWDER

1 PASSION FRUIT

100ML WATER

40G CASTER SUGAR

Spread the batter on the baking paper into a rectangle of about 35 x 25cm. Bake for about 8 minutes. Transfer the sponge with the baking paper on to a wire rack and cover with a second sheet of baking paper to avoid drying out. Set aside and leave to cool.

To make the caramel, put the sugar and water into a pan and bring gently to the boil while stirring. Boil the sugar without stirring until it turns a rich golden brown. Take off the heat, immediately add double cream and butter, and stir. Be very careful; the hot caramel will bubble up and might splash. Pour into a heatproof bowl and set aside to cool.

To assemble the shell, line a 2 – 3 litre bowl with clingfilm. Take your cool Joconde sponge, still on the baking paper, and place it on your work surface with a long edge towards you. Spread the caramel thinly on the Joconde, leaving a small strip uncovered along the far side. Roll the Joconde tightly, starting with the edge closest to you. Use the baking paper as an aid to roll tightly, and while rolling, remove it from the sponge bit by bit.

Cut the roll into slices about 6mm thick. Line the inside of the bowl with a layer of the slices. Push them in place so that no gaps remain, if possible. The edge will be trimmed – it can be uneven at this point. Set aside.

To make the passion fruit and mango Bavarian cream, sprinkle the gelatine over the water and set aside.

Pass the pulp of the passion fruit through a sieve. Reserve some of the seeds for the filling.

Peel the mango, cut off the cheeks and the flesh around the seed. Blend the mango fruit flesh until very smooth. Add the juice from the passion fruit, and some pips if required. You will need 420g of fruit pulp. If you have less, add some water or fruit juice.

Transfer the fruit pulp to a pan, add the sugar and bring to the boil. Take the pulp off the heat, add the gelatine, and stir until the gelatine is completely dissolved and let cool.

Once the pulp has cooled and the gelatine is starting to set, whip the double cream. It should be stiff, but smooth. Don't over-whip or it is hard to fold it into the fruit pulp.

Fold the double cream into the fruit pulp, first one-third of the cream and then the rest. Pour the Bavarian cream into the cake-lined bowl and level with a palette knife or spatula.

Cut a lid out of the Genoese sponge that fits well on top of the Bavarian cream and place it on top of the cream, slightly pressing down and levelling the cake. This will become the bottom. Put the cake into the fridge for at least 2 hours.

To make the glaze, sprinkle the gelatine over the water and set aside. Put the passion fruit pulp with pips into a food processor and give it a short burst but be careful not to destroy the pips. Put the pulp into a small saucepan and add the remaining ingredients for the glaze, except for the gelatine. Bring the pulp mixture to the boil, then remove from the heat and stir in the gelatine until completely dissolved. Leave to cool.

Remove the cake from the fridge. Trim any excess cake around the edge.

To remove the Charlotte from the bowl, turn it upside down on to a cake tray or cake stand. Remove the clingfilm.

Once the glaze starts setting, pour it over the Charlotte to cover it evenly.

Keep the cake in the fridge until you are ready to serve. Store in the fridge and consume within 2 days.

Triple Charlotte Russe

serves 16

FOR THE GENOESE SPONGE
4 MEDIUM EGGS

125G CASTER SUGAR

125G PLAIN FLOUR

25G UNSALTED BUTTER, MELTED

FOR THE LADYFINGERS
3 MEDIUM EGGS, SEPARATED

90G CASTER SUGAR

90G PLAIN FLOUR

15G ORANGE BLOSSOM WATER

ICING SUGAR FOR DUSTING

FOR THE BLUEBERRY BAVARIAN CREAM
250G BLUEBERRIES, FROZEN OR FRESH

60ML (4 tablespoons) WATER

1 X 12G SACHET GELATINE POWDER

40G CASTER SUGAR

200ML DOUBLE CREAM

FOR THE RASPBERRY BAVARIAN CREAM
350G RASPBERRIES, FROZEN OR FRESH

60ML (4 tablespoons) WATER

1 X 12G SACHET GELATINE POWDER

40G CASTER SUGAR

200ML DOUBLE CREAM

This is a multi-layered, rich and colourful cake for special occasions. It takes some effort to make, but as the sponge and ladyfinger biscuits can be made a day in advance the effort can be spread out. It is important with this cake, as with all Charlotte-style cakes, to have enough time and space for proper cooling.

To make the Genoese sponge base, line a 38 x 25cm baking tray with baking paper. Preheat the oven to 180°C fan/gas mark 6.

Put the eggs and sugar in a heatproof bowl. Place over a pan of boiling water and whisk until the egg mix has reached 30°C or has doubled in volume. Take the egg mixture off the heat and whisk until the eggs are at room temperature – this takes about 10 minutes.

Fold in the flour, then fold in the melted butter. Transfer the batter to the prepared tray and carefully even out the batter. Bake for about 8–10 minutes. The sponge should begin to turn golden and spring back when gently touched. Remove the sponge with the baking paper from the tin and let cool on a wire rack.

To make the ladyfingers, line two baking trays with baking paper or silicone sheets. Increase the oven to 200°C fan/gas mark 7.

Whisk the egg whites to soft peaks. Add one third of the sugar and continue whisking until the meringue is smooth and shiny.

In a large bowl, whisk the egg yolks with the remaining sugar until they turn frothy, creamy and pale. Add one third of the meringue to the egg yolks and fold it in. Sift the flour over the egg mixture and fold it in. Add the orange blossom water and the remaining meringue and fold in.

Transfer the batter to a piping bag with a medium plain nozzle. Pipe straight lines of 7cm length onto the baking sheets. Lightly dust the ladyfingers with icing sugar.

Bake the ladyfingers for about 8 minutes until they start turning golden. Leave to cool on a wire rack.
continued overleaf

FOR THE WHITE CHOCOLATE
BAVARIAN CREAM
1 X 12G SACHET GELATINE POWDER

60ML (4 tablespoons) WATER

1 MEDIUM EGG YOLK

½ TEASPOON CORNFLOUR

225G WHITE CHOCOLATE

130ML WHOLE MILK

200ML DOUBLE CREAM

FOR DECORATION
FRESH FRUIT, AS REQUIRED

DOUBLE CREAM, AS REQUIRED

ICING SUGAR, AS REQUIRED

FOR THE GLAZE (optional)
1 X 12G SACHET GELATINE POWDER

100ML WATER

20ML (4 teaspoons) RASPBERRY LIQUEUR
OR SIMILAR

40G CASTER SUGAR

For the three layers of Bavarian cream, timing is essential. Before adding a new layer of Bavarian cream the previous layer needs to be set. This is best accomplished by letting the Bavarian cream almost set before adding it to the cake. This also prevents spills through little gaps between the ladyfingers.

To prepare the fruit pulps for the fruit Bavarian creams, put the blueberries and raspberries into separate pans, add 1 tablespoon of water to each, and bring the berries to the boil. Simmer for about 5 minutes, then leave to cool. Pass the berries through a sieve and measure the amount of raspberry pulp and blueberry pulp. You need 130g of each pulp.

To assemble the sponges, cut a 24cm diameter circle out of your sponge sheet (1cm less than a 25cm springform tin). Place the sponge disc on the bottom of the tin.

Cut one end of the ladyfingers so that they sit around the sides of the tin, with the intact ends level with the top. Place the ladyfingers around the edge, leaving no gaps.

To prepare the blueberry Bavarian cream, sprinkle the gelatine over the water and set aside.

Heat the blueberry pulp with the sugar until it starts boiling. Take off the heat, stir in the gelatine and let it cool. Once the pulp has cooled and the gelatine is starting to set, whip the double cream. It should be stiff, but smooth. Don't over-whip or it is hard to fold it into the fruit pulp.

Fold the double cream into the fruit pulp, first adding one third and then the remaining cream. Pour the blueberry Bavarian cream onto the cake base, sprinkle with some fresh blueberries if desired, and level using a small palette knife. Put the cake into the fridge or freezer.

To prepare the white chocolate Bavarian cream, sprinkle the gelatine over the water and set aside. In a small bowl, mix the egg yolk with the cornflour. Set aside. Break the white chocolate into a heatproof bowl and set aside.

Heat the milk to scalding point. Take it off the heat and pour one third of the hot milk into the egg yolk while stirring. Pour the egg yolk and milk back to the remaining milk in the pan, stirring constantly. Gently heat until it starts to thicken.

Add the gelatine and stir until the gelatine is dissolved. Pour the hot milk mixture over the white chocolate and let it sit for a couple of minutes. Then stir the chocolate until it is completely dissolved, and the mixture is homogeneous. Set aside to cool.

Once the chocolate mixture is cool and starts to thicken, whip the double cream. It should be stiff, but smooth. Don't over-whip or it is hard to fold it into the chocolate mixture.

Fold the double cream into the chocolate mixture, first adding one third and then the remaining cream. Take the cake out of the fridge/freezer. Pour the white chocolate Bavarian cream onto the blueberry layer and level using a small palette knife. Put the cake back into the fridge or freezer.

To prepare the raspberry Bavarian cream, sprinkle the gelatine over the water and set aside.

Heat the raspberry pulp with the sugar until it starts boiling. Take off the heat, stir in the gelatine and let it cool. Once the pulp has cooled and the gelatine is starting to set, whip the double cream. It should be stiff, but smooth. Don't over-whip or it is hard to fold it into the fruit pulp.

Fold the double cream into the fruit pulp, first adding one third and then the remaining cream. Take the cake out of the fridge/freezer. Pour the raspberry Bavarian cream onto the white chocolate layer, sprinkle with fresh raspberries if desired and level using a small palette knife. Put the cake back into the fridge or freezer.

Once the raspberry cream has set sufficiently, decorate the cake by arranging fresh fruit on top of the raspberry layer. If the cake is to be kept, prepare a glaze. Sprinkle the gelatine over the water and set aside. Heat the raspberry liqueur and sugar to about 85°C. Take off the heat and add the gelatine. Stir until the gelatine is dissolved.

Let the glaze cool until it starts to set, then pour it carefully over the fruit. If the cake is to be eaten on the same day, you can omit the glaze and add decorations using piped whipped cream. You can also sprinkle the fruit with icing sugar. Keep the cake into a fridge for at least 1 hour before serving to make sure all the layers are set. Remove from the tin just before serving. This cake must be kept in the fridge. Consume within 2 to 3 days.

serves 12

FOR THE SHORTCRUST PASTRY
300G PLAIN FLOUR

35G GROUND ALMONDS

110G CASTER SUGAR

1 PINCH SALT

180G UNSALTED BUTTER, COLD, CUBED,
PLUS EXTRA FOR GREASING

2 TEASPOONS VANILLA BEAN PASTE

1 MEDIUM EGG

FOR THE FILLING
50G RAISINS

RUM, AS NEEDED TO COVER RAISINS

4 MEDIUM EGGS, SEPARATED

1 PINCH SALT

100ML DOUBLE CREAM

750G LOW FAT QUARK

150G SOUR CREAM

180G CASTER SUGAR

40G CORNFLOUR

1 TEASPOON VANILLA BEAN PASTE

ZEST OF 1 LEMON

Käsekuchen
Cheesecake with Raisins

When I developed this recipe, my wife said, 'Why have you never made such a delicious thing before?!' My answer was that I didn't have the right recipe. I developed this to combine the richness of a 1950s cheesecake with a twenty-first-century method. This type of cheesecake is one of my all-time favourite cakes. The filling is smooth and creamy, and the raisins add a bit of texture. As with most German baked cheesecakes, this one uses quark as main ingredient for the filling.

Put the raisins in a bowl and add just enough rum to cover them. Cover the bowl and set aside to soak, ideally overnight. To speed up the soaking, you can heat the rum and raisins gently in a microwave – don't boil them.

For the shortcrust pastry, put the flour, almonds, sugar and salt in a bowl and mix together. Add the butter, vanilla bean paste and egg. Knead until a smooth ball of dough forms. Wrap in clingfilm and let it rest in the fridge for at least 30 minutes.

Preheat the oven to 180°C/gas mark 6.

Once the dough has rested, line the bottom of a 25cm springform cake tin with baking paper. Grease the sides of the tin with butter.

Roll the pastry into a disc to line the tin. There should be a rim of about 5cm all around the sides. Prepare the pastry bottom for blind baking, using your usual method (ceramic beans or dried beans). Blind bake the pastry case for 25 minutes. Remove from the oven and leave to cool.

While the pastry case is baking, prepare the filling. Put the egg whites in a bowl, add the salt and whisk to soft peaks. Don't over-whip, or it will be harder to fold the egg whites into the mixture. Set aside.

Put the double cream into a bowl and whip until stiff. Set aside.

Put the remaining ingredients for the filling, except the rum and raisins, into a big bowl and mix, using a hand mixer or a stand mixer fitted with balloon whisk, until smooth. Fold in one-third of the egg whites to break up the quark mix – this makes it a lot easier to fold in the remaining egg whites. Fold in the remaining egg whites. Finally, fold in the whipped cream.

Drain the raisins.

By now the pastry bottom should be done and should have cooled a bit. Spread one-third of the filling evenly over the pastry bottom. Sprinkle about half of the raisins over the filling. Add another one-third of the filling, sprinkle over the remaining raisins, then add the remaining filling.

Bake for about 1 hour in the lower third of the oven. Take care that the filling doesn't burn. If it gets dark with some time to go, cover the cake with foil.

Once done, let the cake cool before removing from the tin. This cake keeps well in the fridge for several days. It is great eaten right away but will even be better the next day.

Versunkener Apfelkuchen
Sunken Apple Cake

This apple cake is one of the easiest to make, and one of the most satisfying German cakes. It was a staple at our Sunday 'Kaffee & Kuchen' (Coffee & Cake) events. There wasn't a village fête with a bake sale where there weren't several versions of this cake on offer. The appearance with the cut apple pieces is very typical. But this cake also lends itself to other fruit – it works well with rhubarb, fresh cherries, gooseberries or redcurrants.

serves 12

5 APPLES
(tart, firm, such as Granny Smith)

1 TEASPOON GROUND CINNAMON

120G CASTER SUGAR,
PLUS 1 TEASPOON FOR THE APPLES

125G UNSALTED BUTTER, OR MARGARINE,
ROOM TEMPERATURE,
PLUS EXTRA FOR GREASING

3 MEDIUM EGGS, ROOM TEMPERATURE

ZEST OF 1 LEMON

200G PLAIN FLOUR

16G BAKING POWDER

½ TEASPOON GROUND CARDAMOM

1 TABLESPOON WHOLE MILK

APRICOT JAM OR ICING SUGAR FOR FINISHING

Preheat the oven to 170°C fan/gas mark 5.

Peel, quarter and core the apples. Make about 10 incisions lengthwise in the 'outside' of each apple piece. Put the apples in a bowl, together with the cinnamon and teaspoon of sugar, stir to cover the apples, and set aside.

Grease a 23cm springform cake tin and line the bottom with baking paper.

Put the sugar and butter into a bowl and whisk until light and frothy. Add the eggs one at a time and whisk to incorporate. Add the lemon zest. Stir in the milk. Sift the flour, baking powder and cardamom together and incorporate into the butter and eggs bit by bit. Spread the batter evenly in the prepared tin.

Lay the apple quarters on top (with the 'insides' down, so that the cuts are visible) and slightly press them down into the batter. Bake for about 45 minutes until a skewer inserted into the centre comes out clean. Leave to cool for about 10 minutes, then remove from the tin.

Glaze the cake with apricot jam, or once cool dust the cake with icing sugar.

This cake keeps very well for 4 days in an airtight container and improves in flavour after a day.

serves 12

FOR THE SPONGE
60G UNSALTED BUTTER,
PLUS EXTRA FOR GREASING

80G PLAIN FLOUR

80G CORNFLOUR

3 TEASPOONS BAKING POWDER

4 MEDIUM EGGS

125G CASTER SUGAR

ICING SUGAR FOR DUSTING

FOR THE FILLING
100ML WATER

2 X 12G SACHETS GELATINE POWDER

150ML WHOLE MILK

150G CASTER SUGAR

4 MEDIUM EGG YOLKS

1 LEMON

750G LOW FAT QUARK

500ML DOUBLE CREAM

Käsesahne-Torte

Despite the very similar name, this cake is very different from the Käsekuchen on page 67. Sandwiched between two thin layers of sponge is a thick layer of a cold set filling, which you could describe as a kind of Bavarian cream containing quark. The combination of quark and lemon is found in many German pastries and cakes. Often tinned mandarin slices are added to the quark filling to give the cake some colour, and in that case the top can be decorated with mandarin slices as well.

This cake is very light and has a refreshing mouthfeel. For me it was always tough to decide between baked cheesecake and Käsesahne-Torte (once Black Forest gateau had been ruled out).

The sponge can be prepared the day before assembling the cake. Grease and line a 25cm springform cake tin with baking paper. Preheat the oven to 200°C/gas mark 6.

Melt the butter in a microwave or over hot water. Sift the flour, cornflour and baking powder together and set aside.

Put the eggs and sugar into a bowl and whisk by hand or using a stand mixer fitted with the balloon whisk attachment, until the yolks have become thick and creamy (ribbon stage).

Fold in the flour mixture, then the melted butter. Transfer the batter to the prepared tin, spread it evenly and bake for about 35 minutes until a skewer inserted into the centre comes out clean. Let the sponge cool in the tin for 10 minutes, then remove it from the tin and let it cool completely.

Once you are ready to assemble the cake, make sure you have enough space in your fridge for the cake. Cut the sponge in half horizontally so that you get two even layers of equal thickness.

Put the bottom layer of sponge into a 25cm springform cake tin. Now line the sides of the tin with baking paper or clingfilm. Set aside. Put the water into a wide bowl and sprinkle the gelatine over it.

Put the milk, sugar, egg yolks, zest from the lemon and 2 teaspoons of lemon juice into a saucepan and heat until it thickens very lightly. It should have reached a temperature of 85°C at this point. Take the saucepan off the heat, add the gelatine and water mixture and stir gently until all the gelatine is dissolved. Let cool until lukewarm and the gelatine starts to set.

Meanwhile, put the quark into a bowl and whisk until smooth. Pour the double cream into a large bowl.

When the egg-gelatine mixture is ready, whip the cream to soft peaks. Don't over-whip or it will be harder to fold it into the egg mixture. Fold the quark and whipped cream into the egg mixture bit by bit. Add in a bit more lemon juice if desired.

Transfer the filling onto the bottom layer of sponge and spread it evenly. Work quickly because the filling might set. Place the top sponge layer onto the filling and press it gently. Put the tin into the fridge for at least 3 hours, or overnight if possible.

Just before the cake is needed, take it out of the tin, sprinkle the with icing sugar, and mark 16 pieces with either a cake divider or the back of a knife.

This cake keeps for several days stored in the fridge.

Russischer Zupfkuchen
Russian Plucked Cake

The literal translation for this recipe is 'Russian pulled cake'. It is a baked cheesecake with a chocolate shortcrust bottom, and some of the chocolate pastry is pulled apart and sprinkled over the top. This gives the slices a very attractive black-and-white look, and there is a beautiful contrast in both texture and flavour, which you experience with every bite.

serves 12

FOR THE PASTRY
280G PLAIN FLOUR

40G COCOA POWDER

10G BAKING POWDER

125G CASTER SUGAR

1 MEDIUM EGG

150G UNSALTED BUTTER,
ROOM TEMPERATURE,
PLUS EXTRA FOR GREASING

ZEST OF 1 MEDIUM ORANGE

FOR THE FILLING
250G UNSALTED BUTTER, MELTED

500G LOW FAT QUARK,
ROOM TEMPERATURE

150G CASTER SUGAR

2 TEASPOONS VANILLA BEAN PASTE

3 MEDIUM EGGS

40G CORNFLOUR

For the pastry, sift the flour, cocoa powder and baking powder together in a bowl. Add the remaining pastry ingredients and mix with your hands until the dough forms a smooth ball. Wrap the dough in clingfilm and chill in the fridge for at least 30 minutes. While the dough is resting, prepare the filling and the tin. Grease a 25cm springform cake tin with butter, or line it with baking paper.

Preheat the oven to 180°C/gas mark 4.

Melt the butter in a microwave or in a saucepan on the hob. Make sure it doesn't get too hot – it should be lukewarm when being used.

While the butter is cooling, take two-thirds of the chocolate dough and roll it out slightly bigger than the diameter of the cake tin. It should be big enough to get a 2cm rim around the sides. Line the tin with the chocolate dough.

Combine all the filling ingredients in a bowl and whisk until smooth. Spread the filling evenly in the lined tin, ideally not covering the rim.

Take the remaining chocolate dough, pull it into rough pieces and sprinkle them over the filling. Don't attempt to cover the whole area; you get the best effect if plenty of white filling shines through the gaps. Bake for about 1 hour in the bottom third of the oven.

Leave the cake to cool in the tin for 10 minutes, then transfer it to a wire rack to cool completely. This cake keeps very well, and it improves for the first 2 days after baking. Keep in an airtight container for up to 3 days.

Zwetschgen-Kuchen
Plum Tart with Streusel

serves 12

FOR THE PASTRY
250G PLAIN FLOUR,
PLUS EXTRA FOR DUSTING

125G UNSALTED BUTTER, CUBED,
PLUS EXTRA FOR GREASING

75G CASTER SUGAR

10G STRONG VANILLA SUGAR (page 180)

ZEST OF 1 LEMON

1 MEDIUM EGG

1 PINCH SALT

1 EGG YOLK FOR GLAZING

FOR THE TOPPING
ABOUT 1KG PLUMS

75G PLAIN FLOUR

50G GROUND ALMONDS

100G GRANULATED SUGAR

100G UNSALTED BUTTER, CUBED

½ TEASPOON GROUND CINNAMON

This cake used to be seasonal, and always highly anticipated. In our huge garden we had three plum trees, and in some years, they carried so much fruit that the branches had to be supported. Everybody looked forward to the harvest, and after eating the ripe fruit directly from the trees, plum tarts in all their variations were a highlight of the season.

This recipe is quite simple, but very tasty. Depending on the type of plums the tart can get a bit juicy. The amount of Streusel seems small as this cake shouldn't be completely covered.

Preheat the oven to 175°C fan/gas mark 6. Grease and line a 25cm springform cake tin with baking paper.

Put all the ingredients for the pastry, except the egg yolk, into a bowl. With your hands, mix and work the ingredients together until the dough becomes smooth and pliable. On a floured surface, roll out the dough slightly larger than the diameter of the tin. Transfer the dough to the tin – there should be a rim of about 3cm around the sides. Brush the inside of the pastry base with egg yolk.

Prepare the plums. Wash them, halve them and remove the stones. Then, from the cut side, cut them again about halfway through. Arrange the plums on the pastry bottom.

For the Streusel, add the remaining topping ingredients to a bowl and mix and work the dough with your hands until the dough holds together in big chunks. Spread the chunks randomly over the plums, leaving part of the plums uncovered.

Bake for about 1 hour 10 minutes. Keep an eye on the colour of the Streusel and don't let it get too dark.

This cake tastes great warm, and whipped cream or vanilla ice cream are good accompaniments. It keeps well for several days stored in an airtight container.

Johannisbeer-Kuchen mit Baiser
Redcurrant Tart with Meringue

My parents always grew redcurrants in their garden and, like so many other fruit cakes, this was – and still is – a seasonal favourite.

Preheat the oven to 180°C fan/gas mark 6. Grease and line a 25cm springform cake tin with baking paper.

For the pastry, sift the flour and salt together. Add 85g of the sugar, the egg and butter. With your hands, mix and work the ingredients together until the dough becomes smooth and pliable. On a floured surface, roll out the dough slightly larger than the diameter of the tin. Transfer the dough to the tin – there should be a rim of about 3cm around the sides.

Using baking beans, blind bake the pastry case for about 12 minutes. Remove the baking beans and leave to cool.

Meanwhile, whip the egg whites to soft peaks. Continue whipping and add 1 tablespoon of the remaining 200g sugar at a time; whip until the sugar is completely dissolved. Continue until all the sugar has been added. If you rub some of the meringue between your thumb and index finger and you can still feel grains, the meringue will start to ooze liquid after baking.

Divide the meringue into 2 equal parts. Reserve one part, and gently fold the hazelnuts into the other part of the meringue. Then fold in the fruit and spread in the pastry case. Spread the reserved meringue over the top of the tart.

Reduce the oven temperature to 160°C fan/gas mark 4 and bake for about 50 minutes. The tips of the meringue should start turning light golden, and the meringue should sound hollow when knocked gently. Leave the cake to cool in the tin.

This cake is best eaten fresh, due to the meringue getting soggy when the cake is stored.

serves 12

250G PLAIN FLOUR,
PLUS EXTRA FOR DUSTING

1 PINCH SALT

285G CASTER SUGAR

1 MEDIUM EGG

125G UNSALTED BUTTER, CUBED,
PLUS EXTRA FOR GREASING

4 MEDIUM EGG WHITES

100G HAZELNUTS, GROUND

500G REDCURRANTS
OR FROZEN SUMMER FRUIT

Birnen-Kuchen mit Guss Pear Tart with Sour Cream

This tart combines moist, soft pears and a rich, custard-like filling with a chocolate shortcrust pastry that is not too sweet. A very satisfying and classic combination.

serves 12

200G PLAIN FLOUR

50G COCOA POWDER

1 PINCH SALT

125G CASTER SUGAR

3 MEDIUM EGGS

125G UNSALTED BUTTER, CUBED, PLUS EXTRA FOR GREASING

4 PEARS, RIPE, BUT FIRM

60G GROUND ALMONDS

300G SOUR CREAM

¼ TEASPOON GROUND CARDAMOM

¼ TEASPOON GROUND NUTMEG

Preheat the oven to 200°C fan/gas mark 7. Line and grease a 25cm springform cake tin with baking paper.

For the pastry, sift the flour, cocoa powder and salt together. Add 85g of the sugar, 1 egg and the butter. With your hands, mix and work the ingredients together until the dough becomes smooth and pliable. On a floured surface, roll out the dough slightly larger than the diameter of the tin. Transfer the pastry to the tin – there should be a rim of about 3cm around the sides.

Using baking beans, blind bake the pastry case for about 12 minutes. Remove from the oven and reduce the temperature to 170°C fan/gas mark 5.

While the pastry case is baking, peel the pears, cut them in half lengthwise and remove the cores.

Sprinkle the cake bottom with ground almonds. Place the eight pear halves, cut-side down, on top of the almonds. It might be necessary to trim the pears a bit.

For the filling, put the sour cream, 2 remaining eggs, the remaining 40g sugar and the spices into a bowl and whisk until evenly distributed. Pour the filling over the pears. Do not overfill the tart – there should be no spill over the edge.

Bake the tart for about 50 minutes. The filling will still be a light colour, but darker patches will start showing. Leave to cool before eating. This tart keeps in an airtight container for up to 3 days.

Apfelkuchen mit Marzipan-Guss
Apple Marzipan Tart

Marzipan has always been a favourite of mine, and this cake uses it to give a humble apple tart a rich almond flavour and a beautiful creamy texture.

serves 12

250G PLAIN FLOUR,
PLUS EXTRA FOR DUSTING

1 PINCH SALT

75G CASTER SUGAR

90G STRONG VANILLA SUGAR (page 180)
OR VANILLA BEAN PASTE

3 MEDIUM EGGS

125G UNSALTED BUTTER, CUBED,
PLUS EXTRA FOR GREASING

1KG APPLES
(use apples that keep their shape
when baked, e.g. Granny Smith)

20G CORNFLOUR

250ML WHOLE MILK

150G MARZIPAN
(page 189 or ready-made)

Preheat the oven to 180°C fan/gas mark 6. Line and grease a 25cm springform cake tin with baking paper.

For the pastry, sift the flour and salt together. Add the caster sugar, 10g of the vanilla sugar, 1 egg and the butter. With your hands, mix and work the ingredients together until the dough becomes smooth and pliable. On a floured surface, roll out the dough slightly larger than the diameter of the tin. Transfer the dough to the tin – there should be a rim of about 4cm around the sides.

Peel, core and slice the apples. The slices should be about 5mm thick. Spread the slices over the pastry.

For the filling, mix the cornflour, remaining 80g vanilla sugar and some of the milk together to get a smooth, thick liquid without any lumps.

Tear the marzipan into little flakes.

Bring the remaining milk to the boil and whisk in the cornflour mixture. Continue boiling and whisking for about a minute. Reduce the heat and add the marzipan. Stir until the marzipan is completely dissolved. Remove from the heat and leave to cool. Once lukewarm, whisk in the remaining 2 eggs. Pour the filling over the apples and spread evenly.

Bake for about 50 minutes. The filling might get some variation in colour, depending on the distribution of the apples.

Leave the cake to cool for 30 minutes, then remove from the tin to cool completely. This cake is best on the second day, and it keeps for 3–4 days in an airtight container.

serves 12

240G PLAIN FLOUR,
PLUS EXTRA FOR DUSTING

20G COCOA POWDER

200G UNSALTED BUTTER, COLD, CUBED,
PLUS EXTRA FOR GREASING

175G CASTER SUGAR

200G NUTS, GROUND
(hazelnuts or almonds, with skin on)

1½ TEASPOONS GROUND CINNAMON

¼ TEASPOON GROUND CLOVES

1 MEDIUM EGG

1 TABLESPOON KIRSCH

400G RASPBERRY JAM

1 EGG YOLK FOR GLAZING

ICING SUGAR FOR DUSTING

Linzer Torte

Every year at the end of November the Christmas baking season was kickstarted in our house by making Linzer Torte. The small kitchen filled with the smell of cinnamon, cloves, kirsch and freshly ground nuts. My brother and I were always heavily involved. Under our mother's direction we measured the ingredients, ground the nuts and made the dough. This is the best-tasting raw dough you can get!

The usual technique of making this short dough was a bit intimidating to me: the flour, cocoa powder, spices, nuts and sugar are piled on the table, the butter cubes are sprinkled on top. Then a well is made in which the egg and the kirsch go. Using a big chef's knife, the mountain is then repeatedly cut and re-erected. It is a huge credit to my mother that she taught us this method and we never came to harm.

This recipe can be made with the usual, less dangerous, all-in-one method, which I recommend below. This version of Linzer Torte unfolds its full flavour after a couple of weeks in an airtight container.

Put all the ingredients, except the jam, egg yolk and icing sugar, into a big bowl. Mix and knead swiftly with your hands until the dough holds together well. Make a ball, wrap in clingfilm and let it rest in the fridge for at least 2 hours.

Once the dough has rested, preheat the oven to 175°C fan/gas mark 6. Grease a 25cm springform or sandwich tin.

Reserve one-third of the dough for decorations. On a lightly floured surface, roll out two-thirds of the dough until about 1cm thick and slightly bigger than the tin. Transfer the dough to the tin. The dough is quite brittle, and tears are not unusual. Make sure there is a rim all the way round, about 2cm high. You can cut any excess and use it to patch up the rim in other places. Prick the bottom of the cake with a fork.

Apply some decoration to the rim. I use two forks, one in each hand, with the rounded sides facing each other, grab a 3cm stretch of the rim and squeeze it between the forks. Repeat all the way around the rim.

Fill the cake with jam – you should have an even layer, about 4mm thick.

Roll out the remaining one-third of the dough until about 4mm thick for the decorations. If you want to make the classic lattice pattern, cut the dough into strips and place them on the jam. You can also decorate the cake with star or leaf patterns or other geometric ideas. Using a brush, glaze the decorations and rim with the egg yolk, trying not to get egg yolk onto the jam.

Bake for 30–40 minutes; watch the colour of the rim and the egg yolk – the colour of the rim should be brown, like milk chocolate.

Leave to cool for about 10 minutes, then remove from the tin and let cool on a wire rack. Dust with icing sugar to serve.

This cake tastes great fresh, but it improves greatly over time, stored in an airtight container in a cool place.

Marmor-Kuchen
Marble Cake

This cake was a standard on our Sunday coffee table and has a lot of nostalgia for me. It is quick to make, moist and flavourful, and the marble pattern was always fascinating to me as a child.

serves 12–24, depending on tin size. The amounts given are for a loaf tin (950g) or a Bundt tin. For a bigger Bundt tin, double the amounts and bake for 15 minutes longer

FOR THE BATTER
125G UNSALTED BUTTER OR MARGARINE, ROOM TEMPERATURE

2 TEASPOONS VANILLA EXTRACT

2 EGGS, SEPARATED

180G CASTER SUGAR

250G PLAIN FLOUR

8G BAKING POWDER

125ML WHOLE MILK

FOR THE CHOCOLATE BATTER
10G COCOA POWDER

15G CASTER SUGAR

25ML DOUBLE CREAM

¼ TEASPOON GROUND CLOVES

Preheat the oven to 170°C fan/gas mark 5.

Put the butter in a bowl and, using a hand mixer or a stand mixer fitted with the balloon whisk, beat the butter until it is light and pale. Add the vanilla extract and egg yolks, alternating with the sugar bit by bit, and whisk for another 15 minutes until the butter and sugar mix is very frothy and white.

Sift the flour and baking powder together in a bowl. Alternate adding the flour and milk bit by bit to the batter while whisking on a low speed.

In a separate bowl, whisk the egg whites to soft peaks. Fold the egg whites into the butter and flour mixture.

For the chocolate batter, take one third of the plain batter and put it into a separate bowl. Fold in the ingredients for the chocolate batter.

Put the two batters in a greased 950g Bundt tin or a loaf tin, starting with the vanilla batter, then add a layer of chocolate batter and finish with vanilla batter. Use a fork to create the marble effect by pulling it through the layers of batter with a swirling motion.

Bake for about 1 hour; the cake should start separating from the tin and a skewer inserted into the cake should come out clean. Cover with foil if the top of the cake starts getting too dark.

Leave the cake to cool in the tin for at least 20 minutes before attempting to take it out of the tin.

This cake keeps very well for up to a week in an airitight container and for the first 3 days its flavour actually improves.

Zitronenkuchen
Lemon Cake

serves 10

4 MEDIUM EGGS, SEPARATED

125G UNSALTED BUTTER,
ROOM TEMPERATURE

125G MARGARINE,
ROOM TEMPERATURE

175G CASTER SUGAR

8G VANILLA SUGAR (page 180)

225G PLAIN FLOUR
OR WHITE SPELT FLOUR, SIFTED

75G CORNFLOUR

1 PINCH SALT

LEMON ZEST FROM 1 LEMON

3 TABLESPOONS LEMON JUICE

16G BAKING POWDER

½ TEASPOON LEMON EXTRACT

FOR THE ICING
125G ICING SUGAR, SIFTED

4 TEASPOONS LEMON JUICE

I always loved lemon cake – it can be whisked up very quickly and is always satisfying to have with a cup of coffee. This sponge is different to the usual lemon drizzle cake, and it should be moist despite not being soaked in lemon juice. The recipe uses a substantial amount of cornflour, and the remaining flour can be substituted with white spelt flour.

Preheat the oven to 175°C fan/gas mark 6. Prepare a 950g loaf tin by lining with baking paper.

Whisk the egg whites to soft peaks.

Put the butter, margarine, sugar and vanilla sugar in a bowl and whisk with a hand mixer, or with a stand mixer fitted with the balloon whisk, until frothy and light. Keep whisking and add the egg yolks one by one. Stir in the sifted flour, cornflour, salt, lemon zest and juice and lemon extract. Fold in the egg whites. Transfer the batter to the prepared tin.

Bake for about 45 minutes, being careful not to overbake. A skewer inserted into the centre should come out clean. Leave to cool in the tin for about 10 minutes, then turn out the cake onto a wire rack.

For the icing, combine the icing sugar and lemon juice – it should be fairly runny. Spread the icing on the warm cake and let cool completely. The cake will taste best on the second day but will keep for 5 days stored in an airtight container.

Obstkuchen
Fruit Sponge

serves 12

20G UNSALTED BUTTER,
PLUS EXTRA FOR GREASING

80G CASTER SUGAR

2 MEDIUM EGGS

60G PLAIN FLOUR

½ PORTION VANILLA PUDDING
(page 184), COOLED

FRESH FRUIT (no pineapples or kiwi!)

250ML WATER OR CLEAR FRUIT JUICE

3G AGAR-AGAR FLAKES

When we were in a hurry to get a cake ready, this was often the cake of choice. My mother would send my brother or me to the shop next door to buy a pre-baked sponge. Then we were all involved cutting up fruit and making the gelatine glaze. Sometimes we would also make a pudding as in this recipe, which stops the fruit juice from soaking into the sponge.

Laying out the fruit in nice patterns was always fun for us kids, and this cake is a great treat on a hot summer afternoon.

A note about the tin: In Germany there are special tins for this which look like flan tins with a raised centre, so when you turn the baked sponge upside down you have a nice, fluted rim. The fruit sits in that large indentation, which helps to contain the glaze as well. If you don't have this type of tin, a flan tin or sandwich tin will also work well.

The sponge can be baked the day before.

Preheat the oven to 180°C fan/gas mark 6. Grease a 26cm flan or sandwich tin.

Melt the butter – it should be liquid, but not hot.

Put 60g of the sugar and the eggs into a big heatproof bowl and whisk over boiling water until frothy and a temperature of 43°C is reached. Take off the heat and continue whisking until the mixture is cold and a bit stiffer.

Fold in the flour, then fold in the melted butter. Transfer the batter into the tin and spread evenly, taking care not to handle the batter too much.

Bake for about 12 minutes. The sponge should separate from the tin and be golden in colour. Turn out onto a wire rack and leave to cool.

Spread the cooled vanilla pudding evenly over the sponge.

Clean the fruit and cut it into bite-sized chunks if desired. Arrange the fruit on top of the pudding.

For the glaze, put the water or fruit juice and remaining 20g sugar into a saucepan. Sprinkle the agar-agar flakes on top. Bring the glaze gently to the boil, stirring occasionally. Once all the agar-agar flakes are dissolved, remove the saucepan from the heat.

Let the glaze cool a bit before coating the fruit on the tart. Leave the glaze to cool and set. Due to the fresh fruit this cake should be eaten within 1 day.

MY COUSINS WITH ME AND MY GRANDMOTHER. SHE ALWAYS HAD SOME PASTRIES OR ROLLS FOR US, AND SHE LOVED TO ORGANISE BARBECUES AND SUMMER PARTIES IN THE GARDEN.

Sweet and savoury breads and rolls

The reason for starting baking in earnest was my longing for German bread. Almost by chance I found the book *Bread Matters* by Andrew Whitley, which got me going. My son's primary school, with its regular fairs and community gatherings, gave me plenty of opportunities to expand my skills.

I was always intrigued by yeasted doughs or sourdough, and after some research I managed to make bread that looked and tasted just as I wanted. But there were also sweet breads like brioche and diverse braids, and the other German yeasted bakes: my quest for bread opened a whole food universe for me.

In this chapter I am sharing some bakes I enjoyed while I lived in Germany, and which are usually bought from a bakery, as well as some sweet breads we baked at home.

Schwäbische Seele
Swabian Spelt Rolls

On my regular commute to London, I always used to sit in the same area of a specific railway car, as did many of the other commuters. For a couple of years there were three of us software developers at the same table. We got talking, and it appeared the other two were foodies, one of them having worked as a chef. We soon started regular breakfasts on the train once a week; the other two brought cheese and cold cuts while I treated them to a variety of breads!

This of course got noticed by other commuters, and one of them told me of the Swabian Seele (meaning 'soul') he was missing from his time in Ravensburg. They are made with spelt flour, using a very wet, soft dough and a long, slow process. Typically, they are topped with caraway seeds and rock salt. After some research I came up with this recipe, using a pâte fermentée, which is a yeasted, salted starter.

On the day before baking, put all the starter ingredients in a bowl and mix them well. Cover and leave to stand at room temperature for about 2 hours. Then put the starter into the fridge overnight, until it is needed.

On baking day, put the flours, salt and yeast in a bowl and mix to disperse the ingredients. Add the water and all of the starter and mix until all is well incorporated. Knead the dough until the gluten is very well developed. In a stand mixer fitted with a dough hook this can take up to 20 minutes. Check it is ready using the windowpane test (see page 201) – the dough needs to be very elastic but holding together very well.

Transfer the dough to a lightly oiled bowl and leave to prove at room temperature for 2 hours, folding the dough 3 times during the first hour. The dough is ready for shaping when it feels fragile, and when touched and lightly dented, it doesn't recover its shape. There should be some big bubbles.

As these rolls are baked directly after shaping, preheat the oven to its hottest setting well ahead of time.
continued overleaf

makes 6

FOR THE STARTER
160G WHITE SPELT FLOUR

130ML WATER

1G INSTANT YEAST

3G SALT

FOR THE DOUGH
260G WHITE SPELT FLOUR

140G BREAD FLOUR

7G SALT

1G INSTANT YEAST

300ML WATER

CARAWAY SEEDS
FOR SPRINKLING

ROCK SALT CRYSTALS
FOR SPRINKLING

VEGETABLE OIL
FOR GREASING

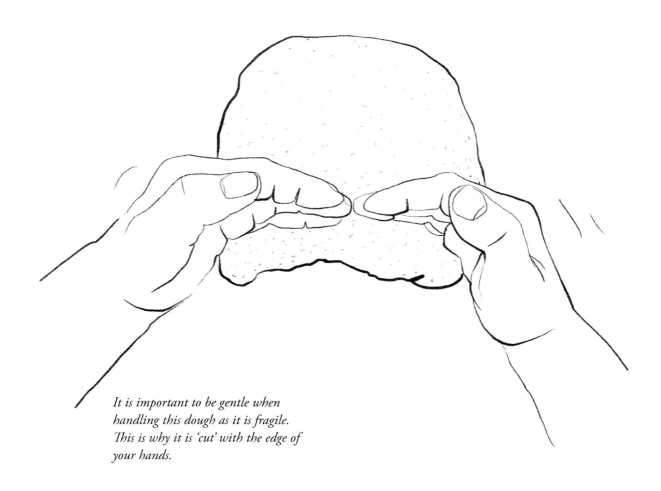

It is important to be gentle when handling this dough as it is fragile. This is why it is 'cut' with the edge of your hands.

Line two baking sheets with silicone sheets or baking paper.

Spread some flour on the work surface to prevent the dough from sticking. Turn the dough onto the work surface and gently pull it to form a rectangle about 2cm thick. Using your hands, fingertips touching and palms facing you, cut an oval piece off the dough rectangle by cutting through the dough with you hands (see illustration opposite). With the edge of your hand on the table, pull the piece of dough towards you so that it folds a bit onto itself and forms a roll with some surface tension. Transfer the rolls to the prepared baking sheet and continue until the dough is used up. The dough should yield six rolls of about 160g. Liberally spray the rolls with water and sprinkle with caraway seeds and rock salt.

Bake immediately for about 20 minutes. To get a crisp crust, spray the rolls halfway through baking.

Eat the rolls filled with BLT, cheese and lettuce, or tomato, mozzarella and basil, or any filling of your choice. These rolls should be eaten soon after baking, as the salt will attract water.

Milchbrötchen
Milk Rolls

Since I started breadmaking in the UK I wanted to replicate the milk rolls we bought in the shop next door when I lived in Germany. They got their baked goods from a traditional baker, Hermann Faisst. At a time when many bakeries adopted time-saving methods and mixes, he stuck to his craft. His milk rolls were simple and unglazed. The crust was thin, golden, covered in little bubbles, and a bit flaky. The crumb was soft and moist. They could be eaten with almost anything, but butter and honey were my favourite toppings. This recipe is as close as I have come to recreating the original.

makes 12

500G BREAD FLOUR,
PLUS EXTRA FOR DUSTING

340ML WHOLE MILK, COOL

6G INSTANT YEAST

10G CASTER SUGAR

10G SALT

60G UNSALTED BUTTER,
ROOM TEMPERATURE

Line two baking sheets with baking paper or silicone sheets.

Put all the ingredients in a bowl. Use your hands or a stand mixer fitted with the dough hook to mix the ingredients thoroughly and knead until the gluten is well developed (see the windowpane test on page 201). Cover and leave to prove at room temperature for about 1 hour.

Divide the dough into 75g pieces. Shape these pieces into balls and place them well apart on the prepared baking sheets.

Prepare the oven for proving – place a roasting tin in the bottom of the oven. Bring about 500ml water to the boil. Place the trays with the dough balls in the oven. Pour the boiling water into the roasting tin and close the door. This will allow the rolls to prove in a moist, warm environment.

After 40 minutes, take the trays out of the oven, empty the roasting tin and put it back in the oven. Bring more water to the boil.

Take a thick skewer or a cake dowel and press it down onto each dough ball to create two halves (see illustration opposite). Press it almost all the way through to the bottom. Use a bit of flour to stop the dough sticking to the dowel.

Put the trays with the rolls back into the oven, pour the boiling water into the roasting tin, close the door and prove for another 40 minutes.

Take the trays and sheet pan out of the oven and preheat the oven to 220°C fan/gas mark 9. Keep the rolls moist by spraying them with water. If you like you can glaze the rolls before baking with milk or egg wash.

Once the oven is hot, put the trays back in the oven and bake the rolls for 12–15 minutes until dark golden in colour. These rolls are best fresh, but can be frozen.

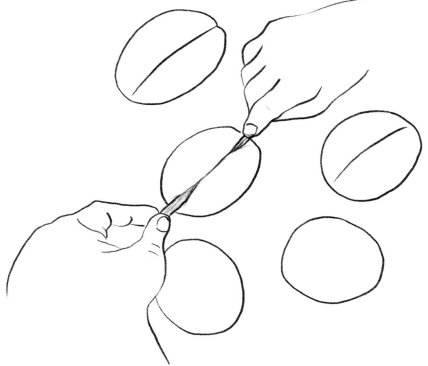

Butter-Hörnchen
Butter Crescents

On those Saturdays when there was no school, or during the holidays, when one of us managed to pop out to the village bakery before breakfast, these fresh butter crescents were always a special treat. Crisp on the outside, fluffy on the inside, they are best eaten by smearing butter on the end and biting it off. Nothing else needed!

makes 6

300G BREAD FLOUR,
PLUS EXTRA FOR DUSTING

175ML WATER, LUKEWARM

6G INSTANT YEAST

30G UNSALTED BUTTER,
ROOM TEMPERATURE

5G SALT

Put all the ingredients in a bowl and mix by hand or with a stand mixer fitted with the dough hook. Once all the ingredients are well incorporated, knead until the dough forms a smooth ball and the gluten is well developed (see the windowpane test on page 201). Cover and leave to prove at room temperature for about 1½ hours.

Once the dough has proved, turn it out onto a lightly floured surface. Divide it into 6 equal pieces weighing about 85g each. Shape the pieces into balls and let them sit covered on the work surface for about 5 minutes, to relax the gluten.

Using a rolling pin, roll the pieces into ovals, about 15cm wide and 20cm long. If the dough gets stiff, move on to the next piece and let the gluten relax. After about 4–5 rolling cycles, you should have thin ovals of the right dimensions. It doesn't have to be exact, but the crescents are better with thinner pieces of dough.

To shape the crescents, starting at the far end, roll up a piece halfway, then stretch the rolled-up part to become about 25cm wide, and continue rolling to the end. You now have a log with a thick middle and thinner ends. Transfer the log to a lined baking tray and repeat with the remaining ovals. (A standard 40 x 35cm baking tray has space for 6 crescents, so make sure they sit well apart from each other.)

Cover with a tea towel or a plastic bag and prove for about 1 hour until the crescents are well risen and feel a bit fragile. Preheat the oven to 210°C fan/gas mark 8.

Bake for 15–20 minutes until the crescents are a rich golden colour. These crescents are great with some butter, or a soft-boiled egg. Best eaten fresh.

Laugen-Brezel
Soft Pretzel

Pretzels, or Brezeln or Brezn in German, are the most iconic German food. Ornaments of pretzels adorn every bakery, and images of them can be found on medieval church windows in Freiburg, where I come from. Often a pretzel works better as a soother for an upset baby than a dummy. They are a part of my upbringing and heritage. And still, there is no better snack after a long shopping spree through my hometown of Freiburg than a Brezel from the bakery at the tram stop. There are many subtle regional differences in shaping, fat content and the use of water, milk, or cream. Here is a standard recipe for a pretzel you could buy on Freiburg's streets.

Disclaimer about lye (German: Lauge): I am giving two options for the finish. One is using lye, which involves a very dangerous chemical, solid sodium hydroxide. The other option uses baking soda, which is bicarbonate of soda, and is not dangerous at all. The results are different in colour and taste, but without a direct comparison the bicarbonate of soda pretzel can stand its ground. If you intend to use lye, I'd recommend baking a few batches of pretzels with bicarbonate of soda, but treat it as if it was lye, to practise the handling and have everything in the right place before starting.

makes 8–10

FOR THE STARTER
100G BREAD FLOUR

2G SALT

⅛ TEASPOON INSTANT YEAST

65ML WATER

FOR THE DOUGH
400G BREAD FLOUR

9G SALT

20G HONEY

5G INSTANT YEAST

25G UNSALTED BUTTER,
ROOM TEMPERATURE

180ML WATER

COARSE SALT CRYSTALS
FOR SPRINKLING

FOR THE LYE OR BICARB DIPPING SOLUTION
2 LITRES WATER

8G SALT

80G BICARBONATE OF SODA
or 80G SODIUM HYDROXIDE PELLETS

Prepare the starter the day before baking. Combine all the ingredients in a bowl and mix with your hand or a spatula until all the flour is incorporated. Cover with clingfilm and leave to stand at room temperature for about 2 hours. Then put the starter in the fridge overnight until you need it – it will be good to use for up to 3 days.

About 1 hour before making the main dough, take the starter out of the fridge.

To make the main dough, combine all the dough ingredients (except the salt crystals) and the starter in a bowl and mix with your hand or a spatula. The resulting dough will be very stiff. Knead the dough on a work surface for about 10 minutes. Don't use any additional flour, you won't need it anyway. The resulting dough should be smooth and a bit elastic. Put the dough into a bowl, cover and prove at room temperature for about 2 hours. Fold the dough once after 1 hour.
continued overleaf

Meanwhile, prepare the dipping solution. Use a big stainless-steel pan and stainless-steel spoons for dipping. Cover your normal work surfaces in case lye spills. When dipping, keep the baking sheets very close to the lye pan and the oven. Always wear protective gloves and goggles when working with sodium hydroxide and lye. Never ever touch sodium hydroxide pellets with your skin.

If using bicarbonate of soda, bring the water to boil. Switch off the heat, add the salt and stir. Then add the bicarbonate of soda – there will be a bit of frothing and splashing, so be careful. Leave to cool.

If using sodium hydroxide, put the water in the pan and then add the sodium hydroxide pellets. Sodium hydroxide creates a lot of heat when it dissolves.

Once the dough has proved, divide it into pieces weighing 85g each. Roll each piece of dough into a cylinder. Once all the pieces have been rolled, start again with the first piece, to roll it into a long strand with thin ends and a belly in the middle. Aim for a length of 60cm. Make sure you don't tear your strands – if there is too much resistance in the dough, move on to the next strand. You will need several cycles to reach the length required.

Now shape the pretzels – the bakers use a slinging method, but there is a simpler, slower way to do this (see photos). Make sure the ends of the little arms are well attached to the middle bit.

Place the pretzels onto lined baking trays, cover and leave to prove at room temperature for about 45 minutes. Uncover the pretzels and put them in the fridge for 30 minutes, so that a skin can form.

Preheat the oven to 230°C fan/gas mark 9.

Take the pretzels out of the fridge. Dip each pretzel in lye or sodium carbonate solution for about 5 seconds. Transfer the pretzel back onto the lined baking sheet. One sheet will hold 4–5 pretzels. Once the sheet is full, slash the thickest part of the pretzels with a sharp serrated knife and sprinkle with salt crystals. Transfer to the oven immediately and bake for 12–15 minutes. Leave to cool on a wire rack. Repeat with the remaining pretzels.

Because of the salt these pretzels are best eaten fresh.

Flammkuchen
Flame Cake

serves 6

FOR THE DOUGH
500G BREAD FLOUR

75ML VEGETABLE OIL

310ML WATER

5G SALT

FOR THE TOPPINGS
CRÈME FRAÎCHE
OR SOUR CREAM AS NEEDED

SALT AS NEEDED

GROUND NUTMEG AS NEEDED

BLACK PEPPER, GROUND AS NEEDED

RED ONIONS, THINLY SLICED AS NEEDED

LARDONS AS NEEDED

CINNAMON SUGAR AS NEEDED
(page 181, for sweet toppings)

APPLE SLICES AS NEEDED
(for sweet toppings)

For some time during my years at university I played music with a teacher from the Ortenau area, near Offenburg and Strasburg. She often organized courses, and on one of those music courses we all went to a country pub. I learned that Flammkuchen was in season. In the area, Flammkuchen used to be only served through the time of the wine harvest. The pubs were booked weeks in advance. And once you arrived at the pub, you ordered by the square metre!

The crisp base, in combination with the simple toppings, is an incredibly sensuous match, and it is no wonder that Flammkuchen or tarte flambée is now almost universally available. There are lots of recipes out there using pizza dough and different bread doughs. Other recipes that claim to be original Alsatian (Ortenau and Alsace are only divided by the river Rhine and have a lot of similarities) use unleavened dough, and this fact makes Flammkuchen incredibly quick to make.

Mix all of the dough ingredients until well combined. Knead the dough until a smooth ball forms. Leave the dough to rest at least 15 minutes before using it. Preheat the oven to the highest temperature possible, using a pizza stone if you have one.

Divide the dough into portions weighing 150g each. Roll each portion as thinly as possible – if the dough starts to pull back and gets unwieldy, let it rest for a few minutes and move on to the next one.

Transfer the flammkuchen onto a piece of baking paper (you can do the last rolling step on baking paper, to avoid tearing). Cover the flammkuchen base thinly with crème fraîche or sour cream and add your topping of choice. The classic is lardons and onions, with a seasoning of nutmeg, black pepper and salt but plain sour cream with nutmeg is also very tasty. For a sweet variant, try a sprinkle of cinnamon sugar and thin apple slices.

Bake the flammkuchen for about 10 minutes in a domestic oven, or 2 minutes in a pizza oven, until they are getting crisp around the edge. They need to be eaten immediately. The dough can be stored in an airtight container in the fridge for several days.

serves 12

500G BREAD FLOUR

50G CASTER SUGAR

3 MEDIUM EGGS

225ML WHOLE MILK

10G SALT

1 X 7G SACHET INSTANT YEAST

175G UNSALTED BUTTER, CUBED,
AT ROOM TEMPERATURE,
PLUS EXTRA FOR GREASING

100G RAISINS

FLAKED ALMONDS
OR BLANCHED ALMONDS AS NEEDED

ICING SUGAR FOR DUSTING

Gugelhupf

This cake has a very long tradition in Austria, Eastern Europe, France and Germany. The name is possibly derived from the name of a monk's hood. The first printed recipe is in Marx Rumpoldt's cookbook from 1591. There are lots of different spellings, and even more regional traditions when it comes to flavours. But all Gugelhupf cakes have two things in common: first, the mould, a Bundt tin with a specific pattern and a spike in the middle, and second, the base, which is a highly enriched yeasted dough that is very soft.

The Alsace, just across the river Rhine opposite Black Forest, is one of the regions where Gugelhupf is a local speciality, baked in a Bundt tin made of clay. Usually, this variant is not strongly flavoured and not very sweet but incredibly delicious. After a long Sunday family walk it can't get much better than having a slice of Gugelhupf with butter and a cup of coffee!

This dough will be very soft, so a stand mixer with kneading hook is recommended. But it is possible, with patience and stamina, to mix and knead this by hand.

Put the flour, sugar, eggs, milk, salt and yeast in a bowl. Mix and knead until the gluten is well formed. This dough is too slack to ever form a ball, but what you are looking for is a change in texture and shine. The dough will be a bit less sticky. This will take about 10 minutes in a stand mixer fitted with the dough hook. Doing this by hand might take longer, depending on your technique.

Add the butter and continue kneading until the butter is completely integrated. This is the hardest part when hand kneading, but be assured that it will happen, and the result is worth it. Put the dough back into the bowl if kneading on a surface, cover and leave to prove at room temperature for 1–1½ hours.

Add the raisins and work them into the dough, using a spatula.

Grease a 23cm diameter Bundt tin with butter. Line the bottom of the tin with flaked or blanched almonds (one in every groove).

Transfer the dough to the tin, cover and leave to prove at room temperature for an hour.

Preheat the oven to 160°C fan/gas mark 4.

Bake the gugelhupf for 40–50 minutes, depending on the tin you are using as different tins vary considerably in their heat absorption. The cake should be dark golden brown. Cover with foil if it is getting too dark to prevent it browning further.

Leave to cool in the tin for about 30 minutes, then remove from the tin to cool completely.

Dust liberally with icing sugar. Gugelhupf is best eaten within a day of baking.

Hefezopf
Yeasted Braid

'Yeasted braid', or Hefezopf in German, is a classic which comes in all different shapes and sizes. It is probably the food that best exemplifies the fluidity of cultures and national borders in the European past (Great Britain excluded). The two defining words say it all – yeast and braid. They can be very simple, just a glazed braided lightly enriched loaf, or a heavily filled braid made with spiced brioche dough. All sorts of variations exist, which are often local specialities.
You will find Hefezopf and its variations in other countries under different names, such as babka, challah or couronne.

Schweizer Sonntags Zopf
Swiss Sunday Braid

I came to appreciate the Swiss Sunday braid on my frequent visits to Switzerland. This fluffy bread is like the milk rolls (see page 98), but doesn't contain any sugar, which makes it a very versatile companion for all sorts of sweet and savoury toppings. Swiss bakers use a specific flour for this which is called Zopfmehl, meaning 'braid flour'. It is a mix of bread flour and white spelt flour, which gives the dough ideal characteristics for braiding, and will result in a close, but fluffy texture. The spelt flour can be replaced with plain flour if you wish.

Put both flours, the salt and yeast into a bowl and mix briefly. Add the remaining ingredients except the egg. Using your hands or a stand mixer fitted with the dough hook, mix the ingredients until the butter and liquids are well incorporated. Knead until a smooth ball forms and the gluten is well developed (see the windowpane test on page 201). Cover and leave to prove at room temperature for about 1 hour.

Once the dough has proved, divide the dough and braid it to your liking; three-strand braids are classic for this bread. Cover your braid with a plastic bag or a linen tea towel and prove for about 50 minutes. The braid should be well risen and a bit jiggly.

Preheat the oven to 175°C fan/gas mark 6.

Glaze the braid with beaten egg and let it sit uncovered for another 10 minutes. Glaze it again, then bake for about 30 minutes, turning the braid halfway through the bake, until golden brown. Store like bread for several days, and toast if it becomes stale.

serves 4–6

400G BREAD FLOUR

100G WHITE SPELT FLOUR OR PLAIN FLOUR

10G SALT

5G INSTANT YEAST

150ML WHOLE MILK, LUKEWARM

150ML WATER, LUKEWARM

60G UNSALTED BUTTER, AT ROOM TEMPERATURE

1 EGG, BEATEN, FOR GLAZING

Babka
Chocolate Braid

What looks more stunning than the randomly swirling bands of dark chocolate in this loaf of white sweet bread! This style of braiding is known in many countries, and is used with different fillings as well. Always an eye catcher, it used to be a special treat on our Saturday afternoon coffee table. The rich spices and citrus zest in combination with chocolate make this truly a great braid for any special occasion.

For the dough, put all the ingredients in a bowl and, using your hands or a stand mixer fitted with the dough hook, mix the ingredients until evenly distributed. Then knead the dough for several minutes until it has a smooth and silky texture. Cover with a tea towel or a plastic bag and leave to prove at room temperature for about 1 hour. Check with the poke test that the dough is ready (see page 201).

Meanwhile, prepare the filling. Put the chocolate, butter and sugar into a pan and melt over low heat. Once liquid, take the pan off the heat and add the cinnamon, cloves and cocoa powder. It's OK if the filling looks grainy.

Line a 950g loaf tin with baking paper.

On a lightly floured surface, roll out the dough to a rectangle measuring about 50 x 30cm. Spread the chocolate filling over the dough rectangle, leaving 2cm of the far short edge uncovered. Roll up the dough rectangle, starting at the near short edge. Seal the seam by pinching it.
continued overleaf

serves 15

FOR THE DOUGH
190G BREAD FLOUR

140G WHITE SPELT FLOUR
OR PLAIN FLOUR,
PLUS EXTRA FOR DUSTING

6G INSTANT YEAST

1 PINCH SALT

40G CASTER SUGAR

180ML WHOLE MILK

1 MEDIUM EGG

40G UNSALTED BUTTER, SOFTENED

ZEST OF 1 LEMON

ZEST OF 1 ORANGE

½ TEASPOON GROUND CARDAMOM

FOR THE FILLING
100G DARK CHOCOLATE
(54% or 70% cocoa solids, to taste)

60G UNSALTED BUTTER

60G SOFT LIGHT BROWN SUGAR

2 TEASPOONS GROUND CINNAMON

½ TEASPOON GROUND CLOVES

30G COCOA POWDER

UNSALTED BUTTER, MELTED,
OR APRICOT JAM FOR GLAZING

Place the roll on a work surface with the seam facing down and, with a sharp knife, cut the roll lengthwise into halves. Twist the halves together to form a rope. You can do this starting at one end and twist this half of the roll, and then do the same for the other half; this way you don't have to manipulate the whole length at once (see illustration opposite).

Place your hands palm down on the ends and, with a scooping movement, bring the ends to meet underneath the middle of your rope (see illustration opposite). Transfer this into the lined tin, and cover with a tea towel or a plastic bag. Leave to prove for 30 minutes–1 hour until the Babka is well risen and the dough starts to feel fragile; a gentle touch with a finger will leave a dent that only slowly recovers.

Preheat the oven to 170°C fan/gas mark 5.

Bake the Babka for 30–40 minutes.

Melt the butter for glazing or heat the apricot jam with a teaspoon of water. Brush the Babka with melted butter or jam as soon as it is out of the oven. Leave to cool for about 15 minutes, then carefully remove from the tin and baking paper.

Let the Babka cool completely before eating. Stored in an airtight container it will last for 3 days.

Rosinen-Zopf
Cinnamon and Raisin Braid

serves 10

FOR THE DOUGH
190G BREAD FLOUR

140G WHITE SPELT FLOUR
OR PLAIN FLOUR,
PLUS EXTRA FOR DUSTING

6G INSTANT YEAST

1 PINCH SALT

40G CASTER SUGAR

180ML WHOLE MILK

1 MEDIUM EGG

40G UNSALTED BUTTER, SOFTENED

FOR THE FILLING
100G UNSALTED BUTTER, MELTED

CINNAMON SUGAR
(page 181) AS NEEDED (about 100g)

RAISINS AS NEEDED (about 170g)

WALNUT PIECES AS NEEDED (about 120g)

FLAKED ALMONDS (optional) FOR TOPPING

1 MEDIUM EGG, BEATEN

Cinnamon, sugar and raisins are a classic combination. With this filling the braid slices very well, and it won't fall apart when spread with some butter.

For the dough, put all the ingredients in a bowl and, using your hands or a stand mixer fitted with the dough hook, mix until evenly distributed. Then knead the dough for several minutes until smooth and silky. Cover with a tea towel or a plastic bag and leave to prove at room temperature for about 1 hour. Check with the poke test that the dough is ready (see page 201).

Divide the dough into three equal pieces. Dust a work surface very lightly with flour. Using a rolling pin, roll out each piece of dough to a rectangle about 40 x 20 cm. This might be easier if you shape the three dough pieces into long rolls first. If the dough gets too stiff, just wait a few minutes to let the gluten relax and then continue where you left off.

Brush each rectangle with melted butter, leaving a 2cm edge along one long side of each piece uncovered. Liberally sprinkle cinnamon sugar, raisins and walnut pieces over the buttered area. Gently press them into the dough, but not right through the dough.

Roll up each rectangle from the long side opposite the free edge into a log and seal, by slightly pressing the uncovered edge into the log. You should have three similar logs about 40cm long. Lay them out next to each other. Braid into a three-strand braid and seal the ends by flattening them a bit and tucking underneath the braid. Transfer to a lined baking sheet, cover and leave to prove for 1–1½ hours.

Preheat the oven to 170°C fan/gas mark 5.

The braid should be well risen and a bit jiggly. Once the braid is ready, glaze with beaten egg and sprinkle with flaked almonds if desired. Bake for 40 minutes. Leave to cool before eating. Stored in an airtight container this will keep for up to 5 days. Gently toast when stale. Shown on pages 116–117.

Mohn-Zopf
Poppy Seed Braid

The poppy seeds in this braid provide some extra texture.

For the dough, put all the ingredients in a bowl and, using your hands or a stand mixer fitted with the dough hook, mix until evenly distributed. Then knead the dough for several minutes until smooth and silky. Cover with a tea towel or a plastic bag and leave to prove at room temperature for about 1 hour. Check with the poke test that the dough is ready (see page 201).

Meanwhile, prepare the filling. Peel, core and dice the apple; the pieces should be the size of a raisin. Put the poppy seeds in a blender and blend until they have the texture of coarse semolina. Put the ground poppy seeds, sugar, lemon zest and water into a saucepan and boil over a gentle heat, stirring constantly for about 10 minutes. If the poppy filling gets too thick and threatens to burn, add a little more water. The final consistency should be a thick, grainy mash. Take off the heat and stir in the honey and marmalade.

On a lightly floured surface, roll out the dough to a rectangle measuring about 50 x 30cm. Spread the poppy seed filling over the dough rectangle, leaving 2cm of the far short edge uncovered. Sprinkle the apple pieces over the poppy filling.

Roll up the dough rectangle, starting at the nearest short edge. Seal the seam by pinching it. Place the roll on a lined baking sheet with the seam down and, with a sharp knife, cut the roll lengthwise into halves. Twist the halves together to form a rope. Pinch the ends and tuck them slightly under the rope to avoid unravelling.

Cover with a tea towel or a plastic bag and leave to prove for about 1 hour. The braid should be well risen, and the dough should feel fragile; a gentle touch will leave a dent that only slowly recovers.

Preheat the oven to 170°C fan/gas mark 5. Bake the braid for about 40 minutes. Brush with melted butter while still hot.

Mix icing sugar and water as required to get a medium thick icing. Drizzle over the braid once the braid is cool. Store in an airtight container for up to 3 days.

serves 10

FOR THE DOUGH
190G BREAD FLOUR

140G WHITE SPELT FLOUR OR PLAIN FLOUR, PLUS EXTRA FOR DUSTING

6G INSTANT YEAST

1 PINCH SALT

40G CASTER SUGAR

180ML WHOLE MILK

1 MEDIUM EGG

40G UNSALTED BUTTER, SOFTENED

1 TEASPOON GROUND CARDAMOM

FOR THE FILLING
1 APPLE (sour, if you like)

175G POPPY SEEDS

80G CASTER SUGAR

ZEST OF 1 LEMON

100ML WATER, PLUS EXTRA AS NEEDED

40G HONEY

40G ORANGE MARMALADE

UNSALTED BUTTER, MELTED, FOR GLAZING

100G ICING SUGAR

Zwiebel-Zopf mit Mohn
Onion and Poppy
Seed Braid

serves 15

FOR THE DOUGH
400G BREAD FLOUR

100G WHITE SPELT FLOUR OR PLAIN FLOUR,
PLUS EXTRA FOR DUSTING

10G SALT

5G INSTANT YEAST

300ML BEER OR WATER, COLD

60G UNSALTED BUTTER, ROOM TEMPERATURE

1 MEDIUM EGG

ONION SEEDS (optional) FOR SPRINKLING

FOR THE FILLING
1 TEASPOON BUTTER

300G ONION, FINELY CHOPPED

2 TABLESPOONS POPPY SEEDS

½ TEASPOON SALT

2 TABLESPOONS DRIED BREADCRUMBS

This is a savoury braid. I got the idea for creating this when I was thinking about some of my favourite savoury filled breads and I wondered what a savoury Babka would look like. I loved onion-filled bread as a teenager, and more recently I discovered poppy and onion fillings that are used in Jewish rolls like bialys. This braid never lasts long enough in our household to get stale.

For the dough, put both flours, the salt and yeast in a bowl and mix briefly. Add beer or water, and butter. Using your hands or a stand mixer fitted with the dough hook, mix the ingredients until the butter and liquids are well incorporated, then knead until a smooth ball forms and the gluten is well developed. Cover the dough with a tea towel or plastic bag and leave to prove at room temperature for about 1½ hours.

For the filling, in a frying pan, heat the butter, add the onions and sauté for 5 minutes on low to medium heat until they become translucent. Transfer the onions to a bowl and add the poppy seeds, salt and breadcrumbs. Mix well and set aside to cool. The breadcrumbs will soak up excess liquid from the onions during baking.

Once the dough is ready, divide it into three equal pieces. Dust a work surface very lightly with flour. Using a rolling pin, roll out each piece of dough into a rectangle about 40 x 20cm. This might be easier if you shape the three dough pieces into long rolls. If the dough gets too stiff, just wait a few minutes to let the gluten relax and then continue where you left off.

Spread the filling equally over the three rectangles, leaving a 2cm edge along one long side of each piece uncovered. Now roll up each rectangle from the long side opposite the free edge into a log, and seal by slightly pressing the uncovered edge into the log. You should have three similar logs about 40cm long.

Lay them out next to each other. Braid them into a three-strand braid and seal the ends by flattening them a bit and tugging them underneath the braid. Transfer to a lined baking sheet, cover and leave to prove for about 1½ hours.

Preheat the oven to 180°C fan/gas mark 6.

The braid should be well risen and a bit jiggly. Once the braid is ready, glaze with beaten egg and sprinkle with onion seeds if desired.

Bake for 35 minutes. Leave to cool before eating. Store in an airtight container for up to 3 days.

Rosinen-Schnecken
Raisin Swirls

The store next door to our house in Germany sold the very best raisin swirls. The store owner was an apprentice with Hermann Faisst in his youth, the baker who made most of the bread and baked goods that were sold there, and I grew up with. I am not sure I am doing him justice with my recipe, but it comes close. The swirls were flatter than Chelsea buns and had a greater diameter. And they weren't as sweet. I loved unravelling the swirl and eating it bit by bit.

makes about 16

1 PORTION BASIC YEASTED SWEET DOUGH
(page 194)

200G MARZIPAN OR HAZELNUT PASTE
(page 189–191 or ready-made)

1 TEASPOON RUM

1 TEASPOON WHOLE MILK

200G RAISINS

150G APRICOT JAM (optional)
FOR GLAZING

150G ICING SUGAR (optional)
FOR ICING

Line two baking sheets with baking paper or silicone sheets. Prepare the dough as directed on page 194 and leave it to prove at room temperature for about 1 hour. Check it is ready using the poke test (see page 201).

Soften the marzipan by kneading, then cut it into small pieces. Put it in a bowl, add the rum and milk, and mix with your hands until you have a spreadable paste. You might need a bit more milk.

Once the dough is ready, roll it into a rectangle at least 35cm long, measured from the edge furthest away to the nearest edge. Spread the marzipan mixture over the dough rectangle, leaving a strip of dough about 2cm uncovered at the short end furthest from you. Sprinkle the raisins over the marzipan. Lightly press the raisins into the dough using a rolling pin or your hands. Roll up the rectangle, starting at the short end nearest you. Once you reach the other end, pinch the seam slightly to seal the roll.

Cut the roll into slices 2–3cm thick and transfer them onto the lined baking sheets, spaced well apart. Cover and leave the swirls to rise for at least 1 hour, as they need to be well expanded.

Preheat the oven to 170°C fan/gas mark 5. Bake for about 15 minutes until they are a rich golden colour. If glazing with apricot jam, heat the jam with a little bit of water and brush it onto the swirls as soon as they are out of the oven.

If you are using a water icing, make this to your liking by adding water to icing sugar, a drop at a time and apply once the swirls are cool. These are best eaten fresh.

Quark-Streusel Buns
Quark and Crumble Buns

While I was studying physics, these buns were my go-to snacks. In Freiburg they were on offer in every little bakery outlet, and I would get one and eat it out of a paper bag while strolling through town. The three layers – sweet bread, quark and Streusel – combine beautifully to something simple but delicious with their differences in flavour and textures.

makes 10

1 PORTION STREUSEL (page 192)

1 PORTION BASIC YEASTED SWEET DOUGH (page 194)

PLAIN FLOUR FOR DUSTING

300G LOW FAT QUARK

75G CASTER SUGAR

2 MEDIUM EGG YOLK

1 TEASPOON VANILLA BEAN PASTE

ICING SUGAR, FOR SPRINKLING OR ICING (optional) AS NEEDED

Line two baking sheets with baking paper or silicone sheets. Prepare the Streusel as directed on page 192 and set aside to cool in the fridge. Prepare the dough as directed on page 194 and leave to prove at room temperature for about 1 hour. Check it is ready using the poke test (see page 201).

Once the dough is ready, divide it into 85g pieces and shape them to rounds. Place the rounds on a floured surface and cover with a tea towel or a plastic bag and leave to prove at room temperature for 30–45 minutes.

Flatten the rounds into ovals about 1cm thick, using a rolling pin. Transfer to the baking sheets, cover and leave to prove again for about 30 minutes. Preheat the oven to 170°C fan/gas mark 5.

Prepare the filling. Put the quark, sugar, egg yolks and vanilla bean paste in a bowl and whisk until the sugar has dissolved.

Once the ovals have proved, make an indentation in the middle using your fist or the back of a ladle. Fill the indentation with quark filling (about 2 tablespoons per bun); there should be a bit of a border of dough visible (about 5mm) so that the filling doesn't spill out during baking. Sprinkle the Streusel over the filling so that it is mostly covered.

Bake the buns for about 18 minutes until the Streusel starts to colour. Transfer to a wire rack to cool. If you want them extra sweet, sprinkle with icing sugar or brush with a stiff icing. To make a stiff icing, sift icing sugar and add water drop by drop while stirring until the icing reaches the desired consistency. These buns are best eaten on the day of baking, but they keep for a couple of days stored in an airtight container.

Pudding-Plunder Custard Danish

There are many things that can be done with Plunder (Danish pastry) dough, but to my mother and me, one of the tastiest is this recipe, which is sometimes also called Pudding-Brezel or Kopenhagener. A long strand of Plunder dough encircles two big 'eyes' of vanilla pudding.

Prepare the Plunder dough as directed on page 197. Prepare the vanilla pudding as directed on page 185. Line two baking sheets with baking paper.

Once the Plunder dough is ready, roll it out to a rectangle about 50cm long, and 3mm thick. This might be easier if you divide the dough into two portions. Cut the rectangle lengthwise into strips about 1.5cm wide. Take one strip and twist it. Shape the twisted strip into a goggles shape. Transfer the shape onto a lined baking sheet. You will be able to place 4–6 Pudding-Plunders on one baking sheet.

Fill the pastry shape with vanilla pudding. Cover the Plunders and leave them to prove for 30 to 60 minutes, depending on room temperature, until they are well puffed up and fragile.

Meanwhile, preheat the oven to 180°C fan/gas mark 6.

Bake for about 15 minutes until the pastry is dark golden and the puddings start to catch.

Put the apricot jam if using in a saucepan with a splash of water and bring to the boil. Then quickly brush the hot pastries, but not the pudding, with jam.

Leave to cool completely before removing from the baking paper, otherwise the vanilla pudding will run. These are best eaten fresh, but they will keep for a day in an airtight container.

makes 8–16 depending on size

1 PORTION PLUNDER DOUGH
(page 197)

1 PORTION VANILLA PUDDING WITH EGG
(page 185)

100G APRICOT JAM (optional)

Apfel-Plunder
Apple Turnover

This treat is very easy to make and can serve as a starting point for many experiments. But it is delicious just as it is.

makes 8–12

1 PORTION PLUNDER DOUGH
(page 197)

5 APPLES

100G RAISINS

2 TABLESPOONS CINNAMON SUGAR
(page 181)

100G APRICOT JAM

Prepare the Plunder dough as directed on page 197.

Peel, core and finely cube the apples. Mix the apple cubes, raisins and cinnamon sugar in a bowl and leave to marinate for 30 minutes.

Line two baking sheets with baking paper.

Once the Plunder dough is ready, roll it out to a rectangle about 40cm long and 3mm thick. This might be easier if you divide the dough into two portions.

Cut the rectangle into 10cm squares. Place about 1 tablespoon of apple filling in the centre of each square. Fold two opposing corners of the square over the apple filling.

Transfer the Plunders onto the lined baking sheets. Cover and leave to prove for 1–1½ hours until puffy and fragile.

Meanwhile, preheat the oven to 180°C fan/gas mark 6.

Bake for about 15 minutes until the pastry is dark golden.

Put the apricot jam in a saucepan with a splash of water and bring to the boil. Then quickly brush the hot pastries with jam. These are best eaten fresh, but will keep for a day in an airtight container.

Zwiebelkuchen
Onion Tart

Variations of this savoury tart can be found in various areas of Germany; in the south-west of Germany it is a village fête staple. In the Black Forest it is usually topped with the famous, finely chopped, smoked and cured bacon, but smoked bacon lardons will do, and for a vegetarian version it is no problem to avoid the bacon completely, bringing the sweet flavours of the onions to the fore.

For the dough, put the flour, yeast, salt, sugar and milk into a bowl and mix together. If using a stand mixer, knead the dough until a smooth ball forms. If kneading by hand, turn the contents of your bowl out onto a work surface and knead until the dough starts to become smooth and shows some gluten development. Full gluten development is not necessary – a cake-like texture is welcome. Add the butter and knead it in. Cover the dough and leave it to prove at room temperature for at least 1 hour until puffy and well risen.

Preheat the oven to 200°C fan/gas mark 7. Grease a 23cm springform cake tin with butter. Roll out the dough into a disc slightly bigger than the tin. Line the tin with the dough – there should be a 1cm rim all the way round. Cover and set aside.

In a big frying pan, heat the butter and add the onions. Sauté the onions for about 5 minutes on a low to medium heat until they have become translucent. Sprinkle the onions with the flour and continue frying for a minute while stirring. Transfer the onions onto a flat dish and leave to cool.

Once the onions have cooled (lukewarm is OK), whisk the double cream and eggs together. Transfer the onions to a bowl and add the egg and cream mixture. Season with salt, pepper and nutmeg.

Once the yeasted base is ready – it should have risen a bit and feel tender to the touch – add the filling and spread evenly. Try to keep the rim of the dough uncovered, so that the filling won't spill over. Sprinkle over the caraway seeds and lardons (if desired).

Bake for about 45 minutes until the crust becomes a medium to dark golden brown. Zwiebelkuchen can be eaten warm, and it goes very well with a hearty drink.

serves 12

FOR THE DOUGH
250G BREAD FLOUR

7G INSTANT YEAST

5G SALT

5G CASTER SUGAR

150ML WHOLE MILK, LUKEWARM

50G UNSALTED BUTTER, SOFTENED,
ROOM TEMPERATURE,
PLUS EXTRA FOR GREASING

FOR THE TOPPING
50G UNSALTED BUTTER

500G WHITE ONIONS, CHOPPED

1 TABLESPOON BREAD FLOUR

100ML DOUBLE CREAM

2 MEDIUM EGGS

SALT, PEPPER AND NUTMEG TO TASTE

1 TABLESPOON CARAWAY SEEDS

75G LARDONS (optional)

Kirsch-Plotzer
Cherry Bread Pudding

I haven't found a translation for the word Plotzer – it describes a variety of bakes that are like bread-and-butter pudding – but with added fruit. The most widespread variety is Kirsch-Plotzer, which is made with cherries and often uses leftover bread. We had a couple of cherry trees in our garden, and during harvest time my mother would sometimes have a Plotzer ready as an after-school meal.

In Germany this pudding is generally made with whole cherries, including the stones! That way it doesn't get too soggy. But it works well without the cherry stones, too. It is usually served with cinnamon sugar, custard or ice cream.

serves 8–12

360G MILK ROLLS (page 98) OR BAGUETTE

400ML WHOLE MILK

1–1.5KG CHERRIES (fresh or from jar)

3 MEDIUM EGGS, SEPARATED

80G CASTER SUGAR

100G UNSALTED BUTTER, CUBED, ROOM TEMPERATURE, PLUS EXTRA FOR GREASING

30ML KIRSCH OR BRANDY

15G GROUND CINNAMON

¼ TEASPOON GROUND CLOVES

½ TEASPOON GROUND NUTMEG

180G HAZELNUTS, GROUND

Cut the bread into thin slices. Bring the milk to the boil, then remove from the heat. Soak the bread in the hot milk and leave to cool.

Preheat the oven to 170°C fan/gas mark 5. Grease a 25cm springform cake tin, or a similar deep oven dish.

If you are using cherries from a jar, drain them well. If using fresh cherries, wash them and remove the stems. Remove the cherry stones, if desired.

Whisk the egg whites to soft peaks.

Mix the sugar, butter, egg yolks, kirsch, cinnamon, cloves, nutmeg and hazelnuts with the bread and milk mash. If this is very stiff, add a little more milk. Fold in the egg whites. Finally, fold in the cherries.

Transfer the dough to your prepared tin and bake for 1 hour–1 hour 20 minutes, or until the top is crisp but not too dark.

If using a springform tin, let it cool a bit before taking out of the tin.

Kirsch-Plotzer is best eaten warm, but it keeps for a few days in an airtight container and tastes nice cold as well.

OUR NEIGHBOUR'S GIRL AND ME POSING IN FRONT OF A GIANT SNOWMAN IN OUR BACKYARD. MY GRANDPA ALWAYS MADE SNOWMEN AND IGLOOS FOR US KIDS DURING WINTER.

Festive bakes

*I*n this chapter I present some seasonal recipes, bakes and traditions that we cherished in our family. The big occasion for baking in Germany is, of course, Christmas. Many of the German biscuits and cakes store very well and, in fact, improve over time. So, the four weeks of Advent, which is the time for spiritual preparation for Christmas, is also a time to bake for the festival.

We started baking in our family around the 1st of December. Every Saturday leading up to Christmas, my mother, brother and I would bake several batches of biscuits, which then got added to a huge cake tin. My mother gave us almost free choice of what to make, and we had great joy in looking through cookbooks to find a recipe we would like to bake. Of course, there were lots of mishaps, but they were all tasty. In the end we would have around 12 different kinds of biscuits in that big tin. This chapter includes some of my all-time favourites.

Our family started the New Year by having a giant decorated sweet pretzel for breakfast, and buttered slices were also offered to visitors who came to wish us good luck, as was the custom in our area. The pretzels were made from a simple enriched dough, sometimes with a hint of cardamom and lemon, and they were highly decorated with braids, lucky symbols, sheafs of wheat and the numbers of the new year starting. Initially we ordered them at a local bakery, but as we all grew more confident, we started making our own, and it was huge fun creating all those decorations.

Carnival was a very special time. Marking the last days before Lent, people liked to go crazy and dress up. On Maundy Thursday an evening parade marked the beginning of the feast. Everybody wore pyjamas or nighties, and the brass band led the procession through the village to the town square, where a symbolic transfer of power from the mayor to the fool's guild took place. I am sure I had my first sip of Glühwein on one of those occasions. On Saturday there was the evening event for adults, and on Sunday afternoon the children's party with dressing up, fun games, lots of food and the brass band (I went once as kind of a female spy from The Avengers – wearing my mother's clothes, my aunt's swimming hat and I had a gun in my handbag). On Monday and Tuesday the streets of Freiburg were full of people in fancy dress, with members of the organized fool's guilds in their weird and wondrous costumes.

To provide the energy for all that fooling around, the bakeries were full of deep-fried pastries, such as crullers, doughnuts and the more regional specialities included in this book. My grandma was always the first to treat us to a bag of Scherben, a wafer-thin, crisp pastry.

At Easter all the sweets held back during Lent were suddenly abundant: the stores were full of chocolate eggs and candy bunnies and treats for the egg hunt. As a tonic to all this sweetness most families would bring out a braided Easter loaf, which is not too sweet and filled with raisins and topped with almonds. The recipe I have included is one that we like in our family.

serves about 10

60G UNSALTED BUTTER

250ML WHOLE MILK, COLD

500G BREAD FLOUR

60G CASTER SUGAR

2G SALT

1 X 7G INSTANT YEAST

1 MEDIUM EGG

½ TEASPOON GROUND CARDAMOM

ZEST OF 1 LEMON

1 MEDIUM EGG, BEATEN,
FOR GLAZING

Neujahrs-Brezel
New Year pretzel

Bakeries can make huge bespoke brezeln in their deck ovens, which can be 1m or more in diameter and very elaborately decorated. A brezel made of 800g of dough just about fits into a standard domestic oven. This recipe makes about 900g, so you have 100g of dough to go wild on your decorations!

Melt the butter in a saucepan. Once melted, add the milk and take off the heat. This will give the milk just the right temperature.

Put all the ingredients, except the egg for the glaze, in a big bowl. Mix with your hands or a stand mixer fitted with the dough hook. Once all the ingredients are well incorporated, knead the dough until a smooth ball forms and the gluten is developed. Cover and leave to prove for about 1½ hours at room temperature.

Once well risen, divide the dough into 2 balls – one weighing 800g and the other 100g. Set the small amount of dough aside, covered, in a cool place. This is for the decoration.

For shaping the pretzel, you need a lot of space. Shape the large dough ball into a log. While shaping it is most important that you don't tear the dough. For instructions on how to shape logs, see page 197. If the dough feels like it is fighting you, give it a couple of minutes rest to relax the gluten and then continue working on it – rolling it gently until you have a long, even strand of dough, aim for 220cm length. Line a large baking sheet with a silicone sheet or baking paper (stuck down with a bit of butter) and place the dough so that the mid point of the strand lies in the centre of the baking sheet but close to the edge furthest away from you. Continue shaping the pretzel as illustrated on the pages 136 and 137. Press the ends of the strands slightly so that they bond with the body of the pretzel. Cover the pretzel with a tea towel and set aside, ideally in a cool place.

Take the remaining dough and create the decorations. To decorate, you can use small amounts of dough and braid them. Make the numbers of the year by rolling pieces of dough into a thread, or use cookie cutters. Popular decorations are also little pig shapes, ladders and toadstools, things that in Germany are associated with good luck. Stick the decorations to the pretzel with a bit of the beaten egg.

Once all decorations are applied, leave the pretzel to rise for another 30 minutes or so, depending on how long it took to decorate. All in all, from dividing the dough to putting the pretzel in the oven should take about 1½–2 hours.

Preheat the oven to 170°C fan/gas mark 5.

Once the pretzel is ready, brush it with beaten egg and bake it for about 25 minutes. The colour should be light golden.

This is best eaten fresh, but it keeps in an airtight container for a few days and is also nice toasted. Shown on pages 136–137.

Mutzenmandeln

These are made of an almond-rich pastry, deep-fried and doused in cinnamon sugar. They are roughly shaped like an almond. They can be kept for a few days.

makes 30–50
depending on the size of cutter

3 MEDIUM EGGS

120G CASTER SUGAR

85G UNSALTED BUTTER,
ROOM TEMPERATURE

60G GROUND ALMONDS

370G PLAIN FLOUR,
PLUS EXTRA FOR DUSTING

1 TEASPOON RUM

1 TEASPOON BAKING POWDER

1 PINCH SALT

VEGETABLE OIL FOR FRYING

CINNAMON SUGAR AS NEEDED
(page 181)

Put all the ingredients, except for the oil and cinnamon sugar, in a bowl and mix well using your hands. The resulting dough will be quite soft and a bit sticky. Roll out the dough on a well-floured surface to about 8mm thick.

Use a heart-shaped cookie cutter (about 4cm wide) to cut out hearts. Cut the hearts in half to get almond shaped pieces of dough.

Add enough oil for deep-frying to a deep, heavy saucepan or deep-fat fryer, making sure it is no more than two-thirds full and heat to 180°C. A wooden spoon dipped into the oil should release lots of bubbles. Try with a small piece of dough first – it should fry quickly, with loads of bubbles.

Deep-fry the Mutzenmandeln in batches for 3 minutes on each side until they are a deep golden brown.

When ready, transfer them onto a piece of kitchen paper to drain the surplus oil. While still warm, douse them in cinnamon sugar. These are best eaten fresh but will keep for 3 to 4 days.

Scherben
Shards

With their highly irregular twisted shapes, their surface covered in bubbles and their crispy texture, these deep-fried pastries are just as exciting to look at as they are to bite into. They derive their name from pieces of broken pottery.

serves 6

1 MEDIUM EGG YOLK

2 MEDIUM EGGS

50G UNSALTED BUTTER,
AT ROOM TEMPERATURE

30ML RUM

70ML MADEIRA WINE

400G PLAIN FLOUR,
PLUS EXTRA FOR DUSTING

VEGETABLE OIL FOR DEEP-FRYING

ICING SUGAR FOR DUSTING

Put all the ingredients, except for the oil and icing sugar, in a bowl. Mix with your hands or in a stand mixer fitted with the dough hook until the dough forms a smooth ball. Flatten the dough, wrap in clingfilm and let it rest for 30 minutes.

Add enough oil for deep-frying to a deep, heavy saucepan or deep-fat fryer, making sure it is no more than two-thirds full and heat to 180°C. A wooden spoon dipped into the oil should release lots of bubbles. Line a baking sheet or big plate with kitchen paper.

Cut the dough into six pieces. On a lightly floured surface, roll out each piece very thinly (less than 1mm thick). Cut each one into diamonds about 8cm long. The shapes don't matter too much, as this pastry is always quite irregular.

Deep-fry no more than two pieces at a time for about 3 minutes until they are light golden brown at the centre, with darker edges. Take the shards out of the oil and transfer them to the lined sheet or plate to remove surplus oil. Dust with icing sugar while still warm. Repeat until the dough is used up.

These shards are best enjoyed fresh, but they will keep for 2 days in a sealed food bag or an airtight container.

Oster-Zopf mit Yoghurt
Easter Braid with Yogurt

A braided sweet bread is great food to share on Easter Sunday morning, when family and neighbours visit, and children are preparing to go on their egg hunt. A slice of this braid, smothered with butter, and a cup of coffee, is a simple and great way to start this holiday. But this Easter braid tastes just as good on any other occasion all year round.

Preheat the oven to 160°C fan/gas mark 4. Line a baking tray with a silicone sheet or baking paper.

Sift both flours, the baking powder, salt, vanilla sugar and caster sugar into a bowl. Add the yogurt, milk, oil, lemon zest and whole eggs and mix, either by hand or with a stand mixer fitted with the dough hook. Once the ingredients are well distributed, knead the dough until it starts showing some gluten development. Add the raisins and work them into the dough. Don't overwork the dough. This dough feels extremely fragile and soft, therefore work quickly, and use plenty of flour to avoid stickiness.

Divide the dough into three equal portions. Shape each portion into a long sausage and transfer them to the baking tray, placing the sausages next to each other. Braid the sausages and pinch the ends of the braid together.

Beat the egg yolk and milk together to make the egg wash. Brush the braid with egg wash and sprinkle liberally with flaked almonds.

Bake the braid for about 50 minutes until the braid and almonds have a nice golden colour. Leave to cool. This Easter braid keeps very well, and after a few days still tastes great when toasted. Store in an airtight container for up to 5 days.

serves 20

250G BREAD FLOUR

250G PLAIN FLOUR

16G BAKING POWDER

1 PINCH SALT

10G STRONG VANILLA SUGAR
(page 180)

80G CASTER SUGAR

250G YOGURT

50ML WHOLE MILK

80ML VEGETABLE OIL

ZEST OF 1 LEMON

2 MEDIUM EGGS

140G RAISINS

1 MEDIUM EGG YOLK, FOR EGG WASH

1 TABLESPOON WHOLE MILK
FOR EGG WASH

FLAKED ALMONDS AS NEEDED

Spritz-Ringe Crullers

Interestingly we rarely had this pastry at home, but I have strong memories of seeing them in bakeries around Carnival time when I was little. Here is the recipe to fulfil my longings from back then.

makes 10

225G BREAD FLOUR

185ML WHOLE MILK

180G UNSALTED BUTTER,
ROOM TEMPERATURE

25G CASTER SUGAR

2G SALT

6 EGGS

VEGETABLE OIL FOR DEEP-FRYING

100G ICING SUGAR

WATER AS NEEDED

To make the choux pastry (or Brand-Teig in German), draw 10 circles the size of your rings (about the diameter of a mug) with a pencil onto baking paper. Cut the paper into 10 squares so that each square contains one ring. Set aside. Sift the flour into a bowl and set aside.

Put the milk, butter, sugar and salt into a saucepan. Very gently heat until the butter is melted, then bring to a rolling boil. Take off the heat and, with a wooden spoon, beat the flour into the milk until all flour is incorporated. Put back onto the heat and keep beating – the dough is cooked enough when the bottom of the saucepan is covered in a white, thin crust. Transfer the dough to a big bowl and continue beating until the dough is lukewarm.

Break the eggs into a jug and beat them lightly. Add a bit of beaten egg to the dough and beat until the egg is fully absorbed. Repeat until the dough has the right consistency: it should be shiny and drop off the spoon in sheets, and it should hold its shape well.

In a deep-fat fryer or deep, heavy saucepan, heat the oil to 185°C, making sure the pan is no more than two-thirds full.

Transfer the choux dough into a piping bag with a big French star nozzle. With the pencil side facing down, pipe one ring onto your template. Pipe an identical ring on top of the first ring. Pipe two of these double rings, and then drop them immediately into the oil. Deep-fry on one side until golden (about 1½ minutes). Take the papers out of the oil as soon as they become loose – chopsticks are great for this. Turn the rings over and fry the other side. Once done, transfer them to a plate lined with kitchen paper to drain some of the oil. Repeat this process until you have used all of the dough.

Once the rings are cool, make a slightly runny water icing; sift the icing sugar, then stir in water a drop at a time, until the desired consistency is reached. Glaze the rings. Eat within a few hours.

Fastenwähe

*This attractive roll is a Lent speciality from Basel in Switzerland.
During Lent you can buy it on every corner. The tradition of this roll
goes back hundreds of years; there is an iron tool from the fifteenth
century for creating the characteristic shape. I came across them when
I was in Basel with my musical friends and I fell in love with them.
That is why, after starting to make bread, I tried to make them here
in England, and this recipe is the result. The original recipes use lard,
but butter or goose fat work as well. Goose fat retains the crust and
texture that lard creates. With butter it will be more like a brioche.*

If using butter, melt the butter in a microwave or in a bowl in hot
water. Line two baking sheets with baking paper or silicone sheet.

Put the flour, salt, honey, yeast and milk in a bowl and mix using
your hands, or a stand mixer fitted with the dough hook. Once
gluten starts to form and all ingredients are well integrated, add the
fat. Incorporate the fat and knead until the dough forms a smooth
ball and the gluten is well developed. Cover and leave to prove at
room temperature for about 1 hour.

Check the dough is ready using the poke test (see page 201), then
divide it into eight equal pieces (about 100g). Shape them into logs
or batons about 10cm long. Place four logs well spaced on each
baking sheet. Cover with a tea towel and leave to prove at room
temperature for about 1 hour. When ready they should be puffy, but
not too fragile. They shouldn't deflate when cutting them.

Preheat the oven to 200°C fan/gas mark 7.

Once the rolls have proved, take a spatula about 4cm long with a
straight edge, or a knife. Make two slits into each roll, right down
the middle, so that there is a bit of dough between the two slits, like
this: - - Then make two more slits, parallel to the middle ones, so
there is one slit on either side of the mid-line. Pull the sides of the
rolls, where you made the last two slits, until you get a shape that
is very roughly circular, with four holes in it (see photo). Spray or
brush the rolls with water and liberally top with caraway seeds.

Bake for about 15 minutes until rich golden brown. They are
delicious just as they are. They are best eaten fresh, but will keep for
a day in an airtight container.

makes 6

150G FAT
(lard, goose fat, unsalted butter)

400G BREAD FLOUR

6G SALT

6G HONEY

8G INSTANT YEAST

250ML WHOLE MILK, LUKEWARM

WATER FOR GLAZING

CARAWAY SEEDS FOR SPRINKLING

Spiegelei
Fried egg

As Easter has such a strong connection to eggs, bakers created a 'fried egg' pastry for the occasion, a yeasted bun dusted in icing sugar, with an 'egg yolk' apricot sitting in some custard. Simple as it is, the look and the different textures always make this a seasonal favourite!

makes about 12 buns

1 PORTION BASIC YEASTED SWEET DOUGH
(page 190)

½ PORTION VANILLA PUDDING WITH EGG
(page 185)

PLAIN FLOUR FOR DUSTING

410G CANNED APRICOT HALVES
IN SYRUP, DRAINED

ICING SUGAR FOR DUSTING

Make the dough as directed on page 190.

Make the pudding as directed on page 185.

After the first prove, divide the dough into 80g pieces. Shape those pieces into balls and transfer them to floured trays. Leave some space between them so they don't touch each other. Cover and leave to prove at room temperature for about 30 minutes.

On a floured surface, using a rolling pin, roll the balls into flat, oval shapes about 2cm thick, and transfer them back to the tray. Cover and leave to prove for another 30 minutes.

Preheat the oven to 175°C fan/gas mark 6.

Sprinkle a bit of flour near one focal point on an oval – where you want to put your yolk – and make a depression with a ladle. Fill the depression with 1 tablespoon of pudding. Place an apricot half, cut-side down, on the pudding and squeeze gently. Repeat with the remaining ovals and filling.

Bake for about 12 minutes until the buns are medium golden. Transfer the buns to a wire rack and dust with icing sugar. These are best eaten on the same day as baking.

Bethmännchen

These are very easy to make and able to withstand a long shaping session by children. In fact, these might have been some of the first biscuits I ever made. Being a speciality from Frankfurt, you can get them there all year round. In the rest of Germany they are more of a Christmas treat. Bethmännchen work perfectly well made with gluten-free flour.

makes about 40

100G BLANCHED ALMONDS

200G MARZIPAN
(page 189 or ready-made)

100G GROUND ALMONDS

75G ICING SUGAR

40G PLAIN FLOUR
(or gluten-free flour)

1 MEDIUM EGG

1 TEASPOON ALMOND EXTRACT

1 MEDIUM EGG YOLK FOR GLAZING

Split the whole almonds in half and reserve for decoration.

Line a baking tray with baking paper.

Cut the marzipan into pieces and put it into a bowl. Add the ground almonds, icing sugar, flour, egg and almond extract and knead by hand until a smooth ball forms. Cover in clingfilm and let it rest in the fridge for about 30 minutes.

Preheat the oven to 160°C fan/gas mark 4.

Once rested, shape the dough into little balls the size of a big cherry or a small walnut. You can do this by dividing the dough, then rolling it to two strands to the diameter you want and cutting those strands into appropriately sized chunks. Roll these chunks into spheres between your palms.

Decorate each ball with three almond halves, the tips of the almonds pointing into the centre. Put the decorated Bethmännchen onto the prepared baking tray. Once the tray is full, glaze with egg yolk.

Bake for about 20 minutes – the tops should be golden, while they should still be very light near the bottom. They keep in an airtight container for several weeks.

Butter-Kekse
Butter Biscuits

*makes about 60,
depending on
size of tcutter*

380G PLAIN FLOUR,
PLUS EXTRA FOR DUSTING

50G CORNFLOUR

1 TEASPOON BAKING POWDER

1 PINCH SALT

200G ICING SUGAR

10G VANILLA SUGAR (page 180)
OR VANILLA BEAN PASTE

ZEST OF 1 LEMON

1 MEDIUM EGG

250G UNSALTED BUTTER,
SOFTENED, CUBED

30ML WHOLE MILK

1 MEDIUM EGG YOLK (optional) FOR GLAZING

LEMON JUICE (optional) FOR LEMON ICING

ICING SUGAR (optional) FOR LEMON ICING

SPRINKLES (optional)

FOOD COLOURING (optional)

As children, these were our all-time Christmas favourites and decorating them got me so excited that sometimes the finished article was more decoration than biscuit. The dough is quite soft, which means that children's hands will find it easy to mix. From my experience, the dough is also quite resilient against overworking. Like most German Christmas biscuits, these will be better after a while stored in an airtight container.

Sift the flour, cornflour, baking powder and salt together into a bowl. Add the remaining ingredients except for the optional finishes and mix with your hands or in a stand mixer fitted with the dough hook, until a smooth dough forms. This dough will be very soft. Remove the dough from the bowl, wrap it in clingfilm and put it in the fridge for at least 1 hour.

Once the dough is cool and firm, preheat the oven to 170°C fan/gas mark 5. Line two baking sheets with baking paper.

Roll out portions of the dough on a floured surface, about 3mm thick. Using cookie cutters of your choice, stamp out the biscuits and transfer them to the prepared baking sheets. Apply egg yolk for glazing if desired.

Bake the biscuits for 10 minutes until the edges start to brown a bit. Leave to cool for a minute before transferring the biscuits to a wire rack to cool completely. Decorate the biscuits if desired – there are no limits. Classics are lemon glaze (mix sifted icing sugar with a few drops of lemon juice to get a smooth spreadable consistency) plus sprinkles, and egg yolk and sprinkles (applied before baking).

Shown on pages 152–153.

Marzipan-Spritzgebäck
Marzipan Swirls

As my brother and I liked marzipan a lot, these biscuits, which are a bit like Viennese swirls, caught our eye, and they had the benefit of using an exciting tool: a pastry syringe.

makes about 50

2 MEDIUM EGG

200G MARZIPAN
(page 189 or ready-made)

70G CASTER SUGAR

½ TEASPOON ALMOND EXTRACT

200G UNSALTED BUTTER, CUBED

200G PLAIN FLOUR

50G CORNFLOUR

DARK CHOCOLATE (54% cocoa solids)
(optional), MELTED

COCONUT FLAKES (optional)

Preheat the oven to 180°C fan/gas mark 6. Line two baking trays with silicone sheets or baking paper. Prepare a piping bag with a medium star nozzle.

Separate the eggs. Grate the marzipan, and stir it into the egg whites. Mix until smooth. Avoid incorporating air.

In a separate bowl, mix the sugar, almond extract and butter until smooth. Incorporate the egg yolks until combined.

Add the marzipan mix, flour and cornflour to the butter and sugar and gently mix with your hands to get a smooth paste.

Transfer the dough to the piping bag and pipe shapes of your liking onto the prepared baking trays – leave enough space between the shapes so that they can spread a bit. Freeze the piped shapes for 10 minutes before baking.

Bake for about 8 minutes; the ridges should just start to brown. Leave the biscuits to cool on the trays for a couple of minutes, then transfer them to a wire rack to cool completely.

Once cool, the swirls can be decorated if desired. Dip the ends of the swirls into melted dark chocolate. You can then sprinkle coconut flakes or hundreds and thousands onto the chocolate if you wish.

These biscuits improve greatly over time when stored in an airtight container.

Hilda-Brötle

These got their name from Hilda von Nassau, Duchess of Baden; the Black Forest, where I come from, is part of that county. In other areas they are called by different names – Spitzbuben, Linzer Augen etc. Our village baker made them all year round, about palm size with three small holes in the top, and often my grandmother would treat me to one of them. A smaller version is more specific for Christmas, as given in this recipe.

makes 30–50, depending on size of cutter

50G CASTER SUGAR

150G UNSALTED BUTTER, CUBED

1 MEDIUM EGG YOLK

1 PINCH SALT

10G VANILLA SUGAR
(page 180)

250G PLAIN FLOUR, SIFTED, PLUS EXTRA FOR DUSTING

ICING SUGAR FOR DUSTING

200G JAM
(raspberry, redcurrant or similar, without seeds)

1 TABLESPOON WATER

Preheat the oven to 180°C/gas mark 4. Line a baking sheet with baking paper.

Put the caster sugar and butter in a bowl and whisk until frothy and light. Whisk in the egg yolk, salt and vanilla sugar. Add the sifted flour and, with your hands, mix until you have a smooth, pliable dough.

Roll out the dough on a lightly floured surface until 3mm thick and cut out biscuits with a 6–8cm diameter fluted biscuit cutter. Transfer the biscuits to the prepared baking sheet. Cut out and remove the centres of half the biscuits with a smaller cutter – a big piping nozzle or the screw cap of a bottle work well.

Bake for about 10 minutes until light golden. Transfer to a wire rack and leave to cool.

Once cool, place the biscuits with a hole precisely on top of the full biscuits. Dust with icing sugar.

Put the jam into a saucepan, add the water and bring to the boil. Using a spoon, carefully pour hot jam into the holes in the biscuits. Leave to cool. Store in an airtight container and they will keep for several weeks.

Quark Stollen

serves 20

250G BREAD FLOUR

250G PLAIN FLOUR,
PLUS EXTRA FOR DUSTING

16G BAKING POWDER

150G CASTER SUGAR

100G GROUND ALMONDS

2 MEDIUM EGGS

250G QUARK OR GREEK YOGURT

ZEST AND JUICE OF 1 LEMON

1 PINCH SALT

150G UNSALTED BUTTER, CUBED,
ROOM TEMPERATURE

20ML (4 teaspoons) RUM

100G RAISINS

100G CURRANTS

100G MIXED PEEL

100G UNSALTED BUTTER FOR COATING

100G ICING SUGAR FOR COATING

This Stollen is a great-tasting alternative to the classic Dresdner Stollen – it is flavourful, keeps well and can be eaten right away! And it will get even better over time if you manage to hold yourself back. Greek yogurt or strained cottage cheese can be also used instead of quark. If using cottage cheese, squeeze it through a sieve to get a smooth texture.

Preheat the oven to 170°C fan/gas mark 5. Line a baking sheet with baking paper.

Sift both flours and the baking powder into a bowl. Add the sugar and ground almonds and mix. Add the eggs, quark, lemon zest and juice, salt, butter and rum.

Using your hands or a stand mixer fitted with the dough hook, mix to incorporate all the ingredients, then knead the dough for a few minutes until it becomes smooth and holds together. Now work the raisins, currants and mixed peel into the dough.

On a floured work surface, shape the dough into a rectangle of about 30 x 25cm. Grab one of the long edges and gently fold it over so that the edge comes up to about 5cm from the opposite edge to create the typical Stollen shape. Transfer the Stollen to the prepared baking tray.

Bake for 1 hour–1 hour 15 minutes. The colour should be a dark golden brown.

Melt the butter for coating; it should just be just melted, so do not overheat.

Once the Stollen is ready and has cooled a bit, liberally douse it in melted butter. Leave to cool completely, then coat with icing sugar. This Stollen is ready to eat right away, but it will improve over time if stored in an airtight container. It keeps for about a week.

Printen

Printen are gingerbread-like biscuits that were always present at our Christmas celebrations. There are many versions. The Printen biscuits we had were rarely homemade – they were one of those seasonal goodies where the commercial quality was just so good that there was no point in making them, at least in our household. For us children messing around with shaped biscuits, a piping syringe was a lot more fun than cutting rectangles, as this recipe demands. However, as I found later, these wonderfully spiced biscuits are actually very quick to make.

Preheat the oven to 170°C fan/gas mark 5. Line a baking sheet with baking paper.

Sift the flour, sugar, spices, baking powder and baking ammonia into a bowl. Mix together the honey, coffee and melted butter, then pour this into the flour mixture. Knead with your hands or a stand mixer fitted with the dough hook until you get a smooth ball. If you like more crunch, add the sugar crystals at this stage; the size of crystals should be about 2mm.

Roll out the dough on a lightly floured surface until 6–10mm thick. Cut the dough into rectangles of about 6 x 3cm. Transfer the rectangles to the prepared baking sheet. There should be about 3cm space between the biscuits. If you want to decorate with blanched almonds, apply the decoration now.

Bake for about 11 minutes until light brown with darker edges. Leave to cool and glaze as you wish. You can leave the Printen unglazed, ice them or coat them in chocolate. Egg white works well if you used almonds for decoration – apply the egg white thinly when the biscuits come out of the oven and are still hot.

As with most German Christmas biscuits, these Printen will get softer over time and improve hugely when stored in an airtight container. They will keep for at least 6 weeks.

makes about 30

380G PLAIN FLOUR,
PLUS EXTRA FOR DUSTING

150G CASTER SUGAR

1 TEASPOON GROUND CORIANDER

½ TEASPOON GROUND CLOVES

½ TEASPOON ANISEED, WHOLE

2 TEASPOONS BAKING POWDER

1 TEASPOON BAKING AMMONIA
(or more baking powder)

150G HONEY, LIGHT, RUNNY

75ML COFFEE, BREWED, VERY STRONG

15G UNSALTED BUTTER, MELTED

1 TABLESPOON SUGAR CRYSTALS (optional),
CRUSHED

BLANCHED ALMONDS (optional)
FOR DECORATION

ICING SUGAR (optional) FOR GLAZE

DARK CHOCOLATE (optional) FOR GLAZE

EGG WHITE (optional) FOR GLAZE

Christmas Stollen,
Dresden-Style

serves 20

FOR THE STARTER
250G BREAD FLOUR

7G INSTANT YEAST

250ML DOUBLE CREAM

FOR THE DOUGH
250G RAISINS

250G SULTANAS

250G CURRANTS

100ML RUM

100ML BOILING WATER

250G BREAD FLOUR

500G PLAIN FLOUR

125G CASTER SUGAR

7G INSTANT YEAST

2G GROUND MACE

2G GROUND CARDAMOM

2G GROUND CINNAMON

ZEST OF 2 LEMONS

500G UNSALTED BUTTER,
CUBED, ROOM TEMPERATURE

200G MIXED PEEL

200G GROUND ALMONDS

250G UNSALTED BUTTER, MELTED, FOR COATING

250G ICING SUGAR FOR COATING

The most famous and celebrated Stollen is Dresdner Stollen, now trademarked, from the city of Dresden in Saxony. It is laden with fruit and is made with double cream and lots of butter. For me, it is inseparable from Christmas. Usually, my parents would be given a Stollen as a Christmas gift and it was a real treat on the coffee table. It keeps extremely well and needs several weeks to mature and unfold all its flavours.

For the starter, mix the flour, instant yeast and cream together and leave to stand at room temperature for 1 hour. Then place the starter in the fridge overnight.

Place the raisins, sultanas and currants in a bowl. Add the rum. Pour as much of the boiling water over the fruit as needed to just cover them. Cover with clingfilm and leave to stand overnight.

The next day, prepare the dough. Mix together the starter, both flours, sugar, yeast, spices and lemon zest. Work the butter into this mix and knead. This might seem impossible at first, but it will come together nicely. I like to do this in a 10-litre bowl using my hands. Normal household mixers won't be able to cope with this dough.

Drain the dried fruit and add to the dough, along with the mixed peel and ground almonds, and incorporate into the dough. Again, this might seem impossible, but with a big plastic spatula and a lot of patience it will come together.

With your hands push the dough into a rectangle and fold it lengthwise onto itself. Use a bit of flour if it gets too sticky. You can make one large Stollen or a few smaller ones, but I wouldn't recommend making Stollen smaller than 800g; I find larger Stollen give a better texture. Transfer the Stollen onto a lined baking sheet and leave to prove at room temperature for about 2 hours. The Stollen will hardly rise.

Preheat the oven to 170°C fan/gas mark 5.

Bake the Stollen for 1–1½ hours, depending on size. It should be dark golden brown. If it gets dark too early, cover it with foil. While the Stollen is still hot, brush it with melted butter until it is saturated. Once cool, cover the Stollen in plenty of icing sugar and keep it in an airtight container or plastic bag for at least 3 weeks before cutting into it. It will last for several months in an airtight container.

Shown on page 163.

Zimtsterne
Cinnamon Stars

These biscuits are flourless, which makes them gluten-free. Zimtsterne were my grandma's favourites, and she liked the meringue topping really thick. At home we made Zimtsterne every year; they are quick and very rewarding. A batch can be done in as little as 30 minutes. If possible, use almonds with the skin on and grind them yourself, as this way the stars get a better colour and richer flavour.

*makes about 40,
depending on size of cutter*

250G ALMONDS, GROUND (skin on)

275G ICING SUGAR,
PLUS EXTRA FOR DUSTING

1 TEASPOON GROUND CINNAMON

2 MEDIUM EGG WHITE

1 TABLESPOON ALMOND LIQUEUR OR RUM

Preheat the oven to 160°C fan/gas mark 4. Line a baking sheet with baking paper.

Put the almonds, 150g of the icing sugar and the cinnamon in a bowl and mix together. Add one egg white and the liqueur and knead with your hands until you get a smooth ball.

Dust the work surface with icing sugar and roll out the dough until 1cm thick. Using a star-shaped cookie cutter of your preferred size, cut out stars and transfer them to the baking sheet.

Once you have used up all your dough, prepare the meringue topping. Using a hand mixer or a stand mixer fitted with the balloon attachment, beat the remaining egg white to stiff peaks. Add the remaining 125g icing sugar bit by bit while whisking. Once all the sugar has been added, paint the stars evenly with meringue. The thickness of the meringue is a matter of taste, but it should cover the top of the stars and leave the sides free.

Bake the stars for 10–15 minutes. The meringue should still be white, and the stars quite delicate. They set while cooling, with a slightly chewy texture. These biscuits keep very well in an airtight container and will improve over time. They will keep for at least 6 weeks.

makes 4 big hearts to write on,
German funfair style,
or 40 biscuit-sized hearts

FOR THE STARTER
350G HONEY

50G MOLASSES

40ML WATER

80G CASTER SUGAR

300G RYE FLOUR

100G BREAD FLOUR

FOR THE DOUGH
7G BAKING AMMONIA OR BAKING POWDER

50ML WHOLE MILK

7G BICARBONATE OF SODA

150G BREAD FLOUR, PLUS EXTRA FOR DUSTING

2 MEDIUM EGG YOLKS

10G GROUND CINNAMON

2G GROUND CLOVES

4G GROUND CARDAMOM

4G GROUND CORIANDER

2G GROUND MACE

2G GROUND NUTMEG

2G SALT

2 MEDIUM EGG WHITES, FOR GLAZING

FOR THE ROYAL ICING
2 MEDIUM EGG WHITES

400G ICING SUGAR, SIFTED

LEMON JUICE AS NEEDED

FOOD COLOURING AS DESIRED

Lebkuchen Herzen
Gingerbread Hearts

*You might be familiar with the Lebkuchen hearts you can get at Christmas markets.
In Germany they are a staple at all sorts of funfairs. They have a string attached, so you
can wear them like a necklace, and they are decorated with royal icing and writing,
ranging from 'I love you' and 'for you', to wise sayings, or something cheeky.*

*These hearts have a unique, soft texture, which I love very much, resulting from a
very long process and the use of rye flour. You will need at least four days to make these
hearts – a real labour of love!*

For the starter, put the honey and molasses in a saucepan and heat to 50°C while stirring. Put the water and sugar into another saucepan and gently bring to the boil, stirring. Continue to boil without stirring until the sugar reaches 108°C. Let both liquids cool to about 30°C.

Once cool, mix the liquids together, then add the rye flour and bread flour. Mix well. Put the starter into an airtight container and refrigerate for at least 2 days.

To make the dough, remove the starter from the fridge and let it come to room temperature.

If using baking ammonia, dissolve it in the milk. Add the bicarbonate of soda (and baking powder, if using) to the bread flour. Add the egg yolks, milk, spices, salt and starter and mix well until the dough becomes smooth. Transfer the dough to a lined, floured baking sheet, then flatten the dough and cover. Refrigerate the dough overnight.

Preheat the oven to 210°C fan/gas mark 8. Line two baking sheets with baking paper.

Roll out the dough until 6mm thick, using as little additional flour as possible. Using a

big heart cookie cutter (7.5cm) or templates and a knife (if bigger hearts are required), cut out the Lebkuchen and transfer them to the prepared baking sheets. At this point you also might want to make two holes to attach a string. Lightly brush with egg white.

Bake for 10–14 minutes until dark brown. Immediately after removing the hearts from the oven, brush again lightly with egg white.

Once the hearts are cool, decorate them with royal icing. To make the royal icing, beat the egg whites until they are frothy and uniform. Fold in the sifted icing sugar bit by bit. Add some lemon juice and whisk the icing until it is stiff and bright white. Adjust the stiffness with additional lemon juice or icing sugar. The icing should hold its shape well when piped. Add food colouring to batches of the icing as desired, and pipe your chosen designs onto the hearts.

These Lebkuchen keep very well and should be left to improve for at least a week. They should not be hard and brittle, but rather a bit malleable. Stored in an airtight container these will keep for several weeks.

Weisse Lebkuchen *White Gingerbread*

This is a delicious old recipe with a difference. Using bread flour and caster sugar, the crumb of this biscuit remains white. The rich blend of spices, the texture and the special glaze give it its name.

makes about 30

250G CASTER SUGAR

2 LARGE EGGS

70G ALMONDS, SKIN ON

½ TEASPOON GROUND CINNAMON

¼ TEASPOON GROUND CLOVES

¼ TEASPOON GROUND NUTMEG

¼ TEASPOON GROUND CORIANDER

130G MIXED PEEL, FINELY CHOPPED

250G PLAIN FLOUR, SIFTED

½ TEASPOON BAKING AMMONIA
OR BAKING POWDER

FOR THE FADENGLASUR GLAZE
125G CASTER SUGAR

50ML WATER

1 TABLESPOON RUM OR BRANDY

2 TEASPOONS ICING SUGAR

FOR TOPPING
GLACÉ CHERRIES

ALMONDS

This glaze is called a Fadenglasur (thread glaze) because it uses syrup that is boiled to 110°C, which in German is the Faden (thread) stage. It is a typical glaze for many types of commercial Lebkuchen. You can make the glaze while the biscuits are baking. Use it warm on hot biscuits.

To make the glaze, put the sugar and water into a pan. Bring to the boil while stirring, and then let it boil without stirring until the syrup reaches 106–110°C. Remove the syrup from the heat. Stir in the alcohol and icing sugar. Set aside.

Preheat the oven to 200°C fan/gas mark 7. Line a baking tray with baking paper.

Whisk the sugar and eggs in a large bowl until very frothy – this will take at least 10 minutes. Cut the almonds lengthwise to create almond sticks. Fold in the spices, mixed peel and almonds. Work in the sifted flour and baking ammonia or baking powder. The dough should be stiff enough that it can be handled. Add more flour if necessary.

On a floured surface, roll out the dough into a rectangle about 2cm thick. Cut the dough into strips about 8cm wide. Cut each strip into 2cm wide strips. You will have 8 x 2cm biscuits. Transfer them to the lined baking tray, keeping about 3cm distance between them. Push the glacé cherries and almonds into the tops of the biscuits.

Bake for about 12 minutes until light golden. Glaze them immediately using a brush before transferring them to a wire rack to cool. Stored in an airtight container, they will keep for several weeks and will improve over time.

Makes 10–40 depending on size of biscuits

FOR THE LEBKUCHEN

180G SOFT LIGHT BROWN SUGAR

5 MEDIUM EGGS

40G HONEY

2 TABLESPOONS GROUND CINNAMON

¼ TEASPOON GROUND MACE

¼ TEASPOON GROUND CLOVES

¼ TEASPOON GROUND ALLSPICE

½ TEASPOON GROUND CARDAMOM

1 PINCH SALT

200G GROUND ALMONDS

200G HAZELNUTS, GROUND

150G WALNUTS, FINELY CHOPPED

250G MIXED PEEL

EDIBLE RICE PAPER DISCS
OR SHEETS (optional) AS NEEDED

Elisen-Lebkuchen
Soft Gingerbread

The best Elisen-Lebkuchen are made in Nuremberg. One of the well known Lebkuchen bakeries uses Italian ice cream parlours - lying idle during the cold season - as outlets to sell their Elisen-Lebkuchen throughout Germany. Needless to say, our family were often first in the queue.

The original recipes are kept secret, but I have tried to capture the taste and texture of the finest Elisen-Lebkuchen. This recipe is gluten-free.

FOR A FADENGLASUR GLAZE
50ML WATER

125G CASTER SUGAR

1 TABLESPOON RUM OR BRANDY

2 TEASPOONS ICING SUGAR

FOR A CHOCOLATE GLAZE
200G DARK CHOCOLATE, BROKEN INTO PIECES

50G UNSALTED BUTTER OR COCONUT OIL

FOR A LEMON GLAZE
150G ICING SUGAR

LEMON JUICE AS NEEDED

Preheat the oven to 160°C fan/gas mark 4. Line two baking sheets with silicone sheets or baking paper.

Whisk the sugar and eggs in a large bowl until very frothy – this will take at least 10 minutes. Fold in the remaining ingredients except the rice paper. The batter should be able to hold its shape; if it is too soft, add more ground almonds.

If you are using rice paper sheets, cut them in squares or use a cookie cutter and knife to cut round wafers. The size is up to you, but around 8cm is traditional.

Portion out the batter onto the rice paper discs using a spoon or a piping bag. Transfer to the prepared baking sheets.

Bake for about 25 minutes until dark golden in colour.
If using Fadenglasur, make as directed on page 170. Apply the glaze to the hot biscuits. Otherwise, leave them to cool.

To make the chocolate glaze, heat the chocolate and butter over a bain-marie until melted. Apply the glaze to the cooled biscuits.

To make the lemon glaze, sift the icing sugar into a bowl. Add lemon juice drop by drop and stir until the glaze has the right consistency. Apply the glaze to the cooled biscuits.

These Lebkuchen need to be glazed, ideally with Fadenglasur or chocolate. This way they develop a beautiful texture and flavour when left for at least 2 weeks.

Vanille-Gipfele
Vanilla Crescents

These very short and delicate biscuits were always a family favourite. My grandma used to make them, and we made them in our family every year for Christmas.

They are easy and quick to make, and last very well (if you can resist eating them right away).

makes about 20 biscuits

40G STRONG VANILLA SUGAR
(page 180)

120G BUTTER, UNSALTED,
ROOM TEMPERATURE

120G PLAIN FLOUR

80G GROUND ALMONDS

½ TEASPOON VANILLA BEAN PASTE

100G ICING SUGAR, FOR COATING

Preheat oven to 170°C fan/gas mark 5 and line a baking sheet with baking paper.

Combine all the ingredients except the icing sugar in a bowl and work the dough with your hands until smooth.

Roll the dough into a sausage about 2cm thick. Cut the sausage into 2cm wide pieces. Roll each piece between the palms of your hand to get a tapered shape.

Place the biscuits on the baking sheet and bend the tapered ends to get a crescent shape. Leave about 2cm space between the crescents.

Bake for about 10 minutes. The biscuit should still be pale but start to firm up. Let the biscuits cool on the baking sheet for about 3 minutes, then gently transfer to a wire rack to cool.

Once cool, toss the crescents in icing sugar. Stored in an airtight container they will last for at least 6 weeks.

ME IN THE FRONT GARDEN, THE LITTLE HOUSE IN FRONT OF ME
IN THIS PHOTO IS PART OF MY EARLIEST MEMORIES.

Basics

Certain cakes and other bakes use the same components over and over again. Good examples for this are flavoured sugars – vanilla sugar and cinnamon sugar. In order to keep the main recipes more readable I decided to give these common components their own chapter.

Vanille-Zucker
Vanilla Sugar

makes 200g

VANILLA PODS, SPLIT OR WHOLE,
AS AVAILABLE

200G CASTER SUGAR,
PLUS EXTRA TO TOP UP

In Germany, many baking ingredients are available in standardized little packets, and the recipes often list ingredients like 1 packet of baking powder, 1 packet of vanilla pudding powder, or 1 packet of vanilla sugar. This approach makes the measuring of ingredients quite easy and consistent.

In the rest of the world this is not the case: you may be able to buy those packets in German stores or over the internet, but here is how to make a supply for yourself. Making your own vanilla sugar is very easy, and it is also a great method to store vanilla pods, whole or split, for further use in custards etc.

Put the vanilla pods in a tall jar that can be sealed airtight with a lid. Add caster sugar to cover the vanilla pods completely.

Keep topping up as needed.

Luxus-Vanille-Zucker
Strong Vanilla Sugar

makes 200g

1 VANILLA POD

200G CASTER SUGAR

While the recipe for vanilla sugar makes a well flavoured ingredient, sometimes you will want vanilla flavouring with a stronger punch. In those cases, use this recipe.

You might want to sift the vanilla sugar before use to remove larger bits of vanilla pod.

Cut the vanilla pod into several pieces and put it into a food processor together with about a third of the sugar. Process the sugar and vanilla pod until most of the vanilla pod has been broken down.

Put the vanilla sugar mixture into an airtight jar, together with the remaining sugar and mix. You can use this immediately, and you can keep topping up with sugar after use.

Zimt-Zucker
Cinnamon Sugar

This is such a useful and convenient ingredient to have in the cupboard for countless applications. Sprinkle it over waffles, use it to make apple sauce, to marinate apples for cake fillings, or to fill braids.

Put the ingredients into an empty jam jar. Screw the lid on and shake. Store in the jar and use as directed in your chosen recipe.

makes 200g

200G CASTER SUGAR

1 TABLESPOON GROUND CINNAMON

Apfelmus
Apple Sauce

For this I like to use a mix of sweet and sour apples, but any apple will do. It is a great way to use up apples that go a bit unsightly.

Peel and core the apples. Cut them into chunks and place them in a small saucepan with 2 tablespoons of water.

Zest the lemon using a peeler so that you get big pieces of zest, which you can remove once the apples are cooked.

Add the lemon zest, sugar, cinnamon and cloves to the apples. Cover the saucepan with a lid and place on medium heat. Watch the saucepan as this can easily boil over.

The apples are ready once they are all soft. Remove the zest, cinnamon and cloves. Blend the apples.

Apple sauce can be eaten hot or cold. A portion of apple sauce with a generous dollop of sour cream is a simple dessert in its own right.

makes 200g

5 APPLES

1 STICK CINNAMON

4 CLOVES

1 TABLESPOON LIGHT BROWN SUGAR

ZEST OF 1 LEMON

Pudding

In Germany, Pudding means a style of custard that can range from crème pâtissière to blancmange, with all sorts of flavours. The classics are vanilla and chocolate, and the vanilla version is very similar to powdered custard available in the UK. Hardly anyone makes them from scratch, as 'Pudding Pulver' (pudding powder) is readily available in shops. It is such a staple that a huge number of German recipes online, and even renowned chefs, rely on it as an ingredient.

In our family, set pudding was a favourite dessert, and it was not unusual for my mother to have ready a bowl of freshly prepared, hot vanilla – or chocolate – pudding for me after school. My grandfather loved it, too.

Vanille-Pudding
Vanilla Pudding
(Without Egg)

In Germany this kind of custard is used in many recipes, and those recipes always refer to the standardised sachets you can buy everywhere. The following recipe is a substitute for those.

makes 6–8 portions

35G CORNFLOUR
(or potato starch)

500ML WHOLE MILK

30G CASTER SUGAR
(adjust according to taste)

10G VANILLA BEAN PASTE
(or 1 vanilla pod)

In a bowl, blend the cornflour with 3 tablespoons of the milk, the sugar and the vanilla bean paste. Bring the remaining milk to the boil in a pan. (If you prefer to use a vanilla pod, split and deseed it and add both to the milk.)

Once the milk has come to the boil, whisk in the cornflour mixture. Reduce the heat and simmer for a few minutes to cook the cornflour. Taste to check the flavour – it shouldn't taste of starch. Remove from the heat and adjust the sugar and vanilla according to taste.

Use either as directed or pour into moulds and let it set. This can be kept in the fridge for 3 days.

Luxus-Vanille-Pudding
Vanilla Pudding
(With Egg)

This is richer, and more like crème pâtissière. This recipe uses starch to set the custard and to prevent the egg yolks from curdling. When the starch gets wet and heated its molecules uncurl and interact with the proteins in the egg yolk, preventing the custard from curdling

Split and deseed the vanilla pod. Place both the pod and seeds, or the vanilla paste if using this instead, in a saucepan with the milk and bring to the boil.

While the milk is heating, place the egg yolks and sugar in a bowl and whisk until thick and frothy. Add the cornflour and continue whisking until well combined.

Pour a little of the boiling milk into the egg yolks, whisking as you do so. Once you have a smooth mixture, pour this back into the pan of milk, whisking continuously. Let it thicken and bubble a bit over a low heat.

Simmer gently for a few minutes to cook the cornflour. Taste to check the flavour – it shouldn't taste of starch. Then pour into moulds to set or use as directed. This can be kept in the fridge for 3 days.

makes 6–8 portions

1 VANILLA POD
or 2 TEASPOONS VANILLA BEAN PASTE

500ML WHOLE MILK

3 EGG YOLKS

60G CASTER SUGAR

35G CORNFLOUR
(or potato starch)

Schoko-Pudding
Chocolate Pudding

The chocolate version is surprisingly easy to make, and very delicious on its own. We used to love it with canned fruit, such as peach halves or mandarin slices. While I preferred the vanilla version, my brother really loved chocolate pudding, and it is the same with my brother's kids. To this day my mother always prepares the two flavours when she gets a visit!

makes 6-8 portions

90G MILK CHOCOLATE
OR DARK CHOCOLATE

1 PORTION VANILLA PUDDING
(page 184)

Melt the chocolate either in a microwave or in a heatproof bowl set over a pan of simmering water (but don't allow the bowl to touch the water). Don't let the chocolate get too hot, or it can break and become unusable. It just needs to be melted.

Use either of the recipes for vanilla pudding and prepare as directed.

Once the custard has cooled, stir in the melted chocolate.

Pour into moulds to set or use as directed. Chocolate pudding keeps in the fridge for up to 3 days.

Weinschaum-Crème
Whipped Wine Custard

This custard is a bit like zabaglione, but it has developed independently in Germany. There are many recipes around. The one given here is quite simple and very tasty. You can adjust the amount of sugar depending on the wine or juice you are using.

Place all the ingredients in a bowl. Ideally use a metal one because it conducts heat more quickly. Place the bowl on top of a saucepan of simmering water. Whisk the custard until it gets frothy and thickens.

Take the bowl off the saucepan and use hot to go with Dampfnudeln (page 22) and similar dishes or pour into ramekins. Garnish with fruit and let set. This is best enjoyed within a few hours.

makes 4-6 servings

6 MEDIUM EGG YOLKS

ZEST OF 1 LEMON

2 TABLESPOONS LEMON JUICE

250ML WHITE WINE OR GRAPE JUICE

50G CASTER SUGAR

Marzipan

Marzipan has a long history in Germany, and it is generally regarded as a delicacy. There are well-known brands making marzipan-based specialities all year round in all shapes and sizes. Lübeck is marzipan-town and Lübecker Marzipan is synonymous with the highest quality. All my family love it, and we always looked forward to gifts of 'marzipan loaves' or 'marzipan potatoes' at Christmas. Marzipan is essentially a nut paste consisting of 50 per cent almonds and 50 per cent icing sugar. It is often flavoured with rose water.

Basic Marzipan

This is the standard marzipan that can be used in many recipes in this book. You can use whole almonds with skin (this is the more flavourful option) or ground almonds. Almond flour might have its oils removed and is not suitable.

If you are using whole almonds with skins, you need to blanch them. Put the almonds into a bowl and pour boiling water over them so that they are well covered. Wait for a few minutes until the almond skins come loose, then drain and peel. Discard the skins.

Put the blanched almonds or the ground almonds into a blender and blend until they become a bit doughy. Add the rose water and icing sugar and continue to blend for another 2 minutes. If the paste clings to the sides while blending, turn the blender off and use a spatula to break it up, then continue blending.

Put the almond sugar mixture into a big bowl and knead by hand until you get a smooth ball of marzipan. At this point you can add almond flavouring or rose water to taste if you desire. If the mixture is too dry, add some more almond flavouring, rose water or water; if it is too sticky, add more icing sugar.

Wrap the marzipan ball in clingfilm and let it rest in the fridge for at least a day. It needs this time to develop texture and flavour profile. This fresh marzipan is best used within 1 week, but will keep in an airtight container for several weeks.

makes 600g

300G ALMONDS (whole or ground)

1 TABLESPOON ROSE WATER

300G ICING SUGAR

BITTER ALMOND FLAVOURING (optional)
AS NEEDED

Edel-Marzipan
Luxury Marzipan

This type of marzipan is for direct consumption but can also be used in recipes like Stollen. Its almond content is 70 per cent. You find this type of marzipan in chocolate-covered sweets of high quality.
You can use whole almonds with skin (this is the more flavourful option) or ground almonds. Almond flour might have its oils removed and is not suitable.

makes 450g

300G ALMONDS (whole or ground)

1 TABLESPOON ROSE WATER,
ORANGE BLOSSOM WATER
OR OTHER FLAVOURING

150G ICING SUGAR

BITTER ALMOND FLAVOURING (optional)
AS NEEDED

If you are using whole almonds with skins, you need to blanch them. Put the almonds into a bowl and pour boiling water over them so that they are well covered. Wait for a few minutes until the almond skins come loose, then drain and peel. Discard the skins.

Put the blanched almonds or the ground almonds into a blender and blend until they become a bit doughy. Add the rose water and icing sugar and continue to blend for another 2 minutes. Rose water is the classic flavouring, but orange blossom water works very well too. If the paste clings to the sides while blending, turn the blender off and use a spatula to break it up, then continue blending.

Put the almond sugar mixture into a big bowl and knead by hand until you get a smooth ball of marzipan. At this point you can add almond flavouring to taste if you desire. If the mixture is too dry, add some almond flavouring, rose water or water; if it is too sticky, add more icing sugar.

Wrap the marzipan ball in clingfilm and let it rest in the fridge for at least a day. It needs this time to develop texture and flavour profile. This fresh marzipan is best used within 1 week, but will keep in an airtight container for several weeks.

Hazelnut Paste

This paste can be used as a substitute for marzipan in many places. You can use whole almonds with skin (this is the more flavourful option) or ground almonds. Almond flour might have its oils removed and is not suitable. I like to use hazelnuts with their skin on; it adds a different visual effect.

Put the almonds and hazelnuts into a blender and blend until they become a bit doughy. Add the orange blossom water and icing sugar and continue to blend for another 2 minutes. If the paste clings to the sides while blending, turn the blender off and use a spatula to break it up, then continue blending.

Put the nutty sugar mixture into a big bowl and knead by hand until you get a smooth ball. If the mix is too dry, add some more orange blossom water or water; if it is too sticky, add some more icing sugar.

Wrap the paste ball in clingfilm and let it rest in the fridge for at least a day. It needs this time to develop texture and flavour profile. This fresh marzipan is best used within 1 week, but will keep in an airtight container for several weeks.

makes 600g

150G ALMONDS (whole or ground)

150G HAZELNUTS (whole or ground)

1 TABLESPOON ORANGE BLOSSOM WATER

300G ICING SUGAR

Streusel

In German baking Streusel (the verb streuen means to sprinkle) is used in many recipes. It is typically more chunky than its British counterpart, the crumble.

makes 650g

250G PLAIN FLOUR

200G CASTER SUGAR

200G UNSALTED BUTTER, COLD, CUBED

In a bowl, mix together the flour and sugar.

Rub the butter into flour mixture until you get a lumpy structure. German Streusel is usually quite chunky.

The Streusel dough can be kept in the fridge for a few hours.

Rührteig
Basic Sponge

makes 1 portion

250G UNSALTED BUTTER OR MARGARINE

250G CASTER SUGAR

10G VANILLA SUGAR OR VANILLA BEAN PASTE
(if desired)

4 EGGS (about 60g each)

1 PINCH SALT

500G PLAIN FLOUR, SIFTED

16G BAKING POWDER

125ML WHOLE MILK

Like the classic pound cake, the Rührkuchen (stirred cake) is based on very simple ratios. The amount of flour is higher than in a pound cake or Victoria sponge, which is compensated by adding milk. The result is a sponge that is firm enough to hold up a fruit or Streusel topping. Rührteig is widely used in German baking and for many young home bakers this is the first recipe they have a go at.

Whisk the butter or margarine with the sugar and vanilla sugar (if using) until light and airy. Add the eggs and salt and whisk until smooth. Add the sifted flour, baking powder and milk and stir until all the ingredients are incorporated.

Use as directed in your chosen recipe.

About Yeasted Doughs

Yeasted dough features heavily in German baking – and in many of the bakes in this book. I give a variety of recipes from simple white dough to very loose and sticky, highly enriched dough. The doughs all have four ingredients in common: flour, water, salt and yeast.

The yeast provides the leavening and needs time to do its work. Typically, it takes 2 hours or more until your cake is sufficiently risen to go into the oven but depending on the recipe and ambient temperature it can take much longer.

Wheat or spelt flour provides two things: starch, which makes the bulk of your dough, and gluten, which holds the dough together and traps CO^2 gas from fermentation and steam during the bake. In raw flour there are two enzymes that react with each other when water is added to create gluten. This process can be sped up considerably by adding mechanical energy, like moving the dough or punching it. This is called kneading.

To trap gases properly and create a nice shape, the gluten needs to be organized; imagine the layers of an onion. Kneading can help organize the gluten, and that is why you shouldn't tear the dough, but rather stretch and fold it over itself. Good gluten development is necessary where the dough needs to hold its shape, like in breads and braids. It is not so important for cake bases of traybakes, for example.

I always say that yeasted dough can feel when the baker is frightened – if you don't work rapidly and with confidence, it will stick to your fingers.

Hefeteig
Basic Yeasted Sweet Dough

This basic yeasted sweet dough is very versatile and easy to work with. It can be used in cakes and tarts whenever a yeasted sweet dough is asked for. It can also be made into rolls or raisin buns. Glazing with milk or egg wash will give it a nice finish.

makes 1 portion

60G UNSALTED BUTTER, CUBED, ROOM TEMPERATURE

500G BREAD FLOUR

60G CASTER SUGAR

2G SALT

1 X 7G SACHET INSTANT YEAST

250ML WHOLE MILK, LUKEWARM

1 MEDIUM EGG

If the butter is too cold, add it to the milk and microwave or heat gently on the hob until the mixture is lukewarm.

Put all the dry ingredients in a bowl and whisk to combine. Add the butter, milk and egg and mix together. Then either knead by hand or use a stand mixer fitted with the dough hook. The dough is ready for proving when it loses its stickiness and forms a smooth ball.

Cover the bowl and leave to prove for at least 1 hour until the dough is well risen and is puffy with lots of air bubbles. Many baking recipes mention that the dough should 'double in size' – this is a somewhat unclear instruction, as the doubling could refer to the volume, or simply to the appearance of the dough, and those criteria are hard to measure.

Use as directed in your chosen recipe.

Luxus–Hefeteig
Rich Yeasted Sweet Dough

This version of yeasted sweet dough is richer and sweeter than the basic dough, and therefore it will be stickier and a bit more difficult to work with. Used on its own it will make great brioche buns.

If the butter is too cold, add it to the milk and microwave or heat gently on the stove until the mixture is lukewarm.

Put all the dry ingredients in a bowl and whisk until combined. Add the butter, milk and eggs and mix together. Then either knead by hand or use a stand mixer fitted with the dough hook. The dough is very soft and sticky, and it can be a challenge to knead this by hand, so using a stand mixer is preferable. The dough is ready for proving when it loses some of its stickiness, starts holding a ball shape and its surface gets smoother.

Cover the bowl and leave to prove for at least 1 hour until the dough is well risen and puffy with lots of air bubbles.

Use as directed in your chosen recipe.

makes 1 portion

80G UNSALTED BUTTER, CUBED, ROOM TEMPERATURE

500G BREAD FLOUR

80G CASTER SUGAR

2G SALT

1 X 7G SACHET INSTANT YEAST

240ML WHOLE MILK, LUKEWARM

2 MEDIUM EGGS

makes 1 portion

500G BREAD FLOUR,
PLUS EXTRA FOR DUSTING

150ML WHOLE MILK

30ML WATER

100G (or 2 small) EGG, BEATEN

60G CASTER SUGAR

40G UNSALTED BUTTER, SOFTENED

10G SALT

1 X 7G SACHET INSTANT YEAST

250G UNSALTED BUTTER,
OR MARGARINE FOR THE BLOCK

Plunder-Teig
Plunder Dough

Plunder is a word used in Germany for Danish pastries. They come in all kinds of shapes, and with regional differences. The dough is fairly similar to croissant dough, but softer. As a result, it must be laminated at a slightly higher temperature because the consistency of butter (or margarine) block and dough must be the same.

Put all the ingredients, except the butter for the butter block, into a bowl. Using your hands or a stand mixer fitted with the dough hook, mix well until all the ingredients are incorporated. Then knead until the dough is smooth and shows some gluten development. The dough should be fairly stiff but pliable. Add a bit more water if the dough is too stiff. Shape the dough into a square, wrap it, or put it into a square container with a lid, and leave it to prove at room temperature for 1 hour. Then refrigerate overnight.

Prepare the butter block. Soften the butter by hitting it with a rolling pin. If you use margarine, this should be soft enough.

Shape your butter block into a rectangle the size of an A5 sheet of paper (which is A4 cut in half). To do this you can use a piece of A5 paper. Put it onto a sheet of baking paper and fold the baking paper so that the A5 paper is fully enclosed. Replace the A5 paper with the butter block and use a rolling pin to flatten and move the butter so that it fills the A5 baking paper envelope completely and has an even thickness. Refrigerate.

During the laminating process you need to keep your butter and dough cool to ensure they have an equal consistency, and that the dough doesn't rise and puff up. Make sure the butter block and dough have a similar consistency. Roll the dough to a rectangle of A4 size. Take the butter block out of its wrapping and place it across the middle of the A4 dough sheet, so that the long axis of the butter block rests on the short axis of the dough sheet. Fold the uncovered pieces of dough over the butter block and squeeze them together to seal the pastry and create a seam.

Roll out the pastry in the direction of the seam, about 20cm wide and 80cm long. Now fold the pastry – first fold both ends to the centre line. If the ends are very uneven you can trim them with a sharp knife. Then fold the pastry onto itself along the centre line. This is called a book fold, for obvious reasons.

Very lightly dust the pastry with flour. Wrap the dough in clingfilm and refrigerate it for 30 minutes or so, to let the gluten relax and the butter solidify a bit.

Next, roll out the dough along the long axis, to a rectangle of about 20cm wide and 60cm long. Fold one end to one third over the dough, then fold the other end over to the edge, to create something like an envelope. This is often called a letter fold. Lightly dust the dough with flour, wrap and refrigerate.

Use as directed in your chosen recipe.

Weissbrot
Basic White Bread

This is a simple, generic recipe for white bread. It is delicious, easy to make, and can be baked in all sorts of shapes and sizes, from rolls to braided loaves.

makes 1 loaf

500G BREAD FLOUR

10G SALT

4G INSTANT YEAST

330ML WATER,
AT ROOM TEMPERATURE

Combine all the ingredients in a bowl and mix by hand or using a stand mixer fitted with the dough hook, until all ingredients are well incorporated. Knead for several minutes and use the windowpane test (see page 201) to determine when the dough is ready for proving.

Cover to avoid the forming of a hard skin and leave to prove for 1–2 hours, depending on the ambient temperature and initial dough temperature. Use the poke test to check if the dough is ready for shaping, see page 201.

If using this for another recipe, continue as directed in your chosen recipe. Otherwise, divide the dough and shape as desired. Cover and leave to prove 1–1½ hours.

Preheat the oven to 230°C fan/gas mark 9.

Rolls of 70g each need around 15 minutes, a 850g loaf of bread of needs about 35 minutes. If baking a loaf, reduce the temperature after 15 minutes to 210°C fan/gas mark 8. Keep in an airtight container for up to 5 days.

The Windowpane Test

The Windowpane Test can be used to see if a dough has been worked enough. Pick up a small chunk of dough and stretch it gently in 4 directions until it tears. If just before tearing the dough sheet is very thin and translucent (like a windowpane) it means that the gluten is well developed. If it tears while still bulky the dough needs more kneading.

The Poke Test

Use the poke test after the first prove to check if dough is ready for shaping. Poke the dough with a finger, quick and deep. The hole should stay open and the dough should not collapse. To us the poke test to check if bread is ready to go in the oven, gently touch or poke the bread – it should feel a bit jiggly and fragile, and the dent should only slowly recover.

How to shape a log with yeasted dough

Turn the dough out on a lightly floured surface. With one hand hold the edge of the dough closest to you, with the other hand grab the edge furthest from you and gently pull to get a flat, elongated piece of dough. Don't tear it. Fold the dough onto itself by bringing the far edge to about ⅔ over the dough. Push down this edge. Using both thumbs gently, bit by bit, push this edge and the remaining single layer of dough near you under the folded part of the dough while rolling that part towards you using your fingers. This way you should get a tight roll of dough which you can make longer and thinner by simply rolling it with the palms of your hands on the table. If the roll gets sticky sprinkle with a bit of flour.

Index

Danke
Thank You

The book you are holding in your hands is the result of a long chain of events, and many people and organisations played their part.

First, I want to thank the team at Kyle: Judith Hannam and Emma Hanson for always having an open ear to discuss ideas and for giving me the encouragement to make the book so personal.

Thank you to the magicians who made my recipes look so good: to Maja Smend for her wizardry with light, to Lizzie Harris, Katie Marshall and Maria Gurevich for baking and styling my recipes with great skill and creativity and to Tony Hutchinson, who, with his sensitive choice of props, enhanced the book greatly. Thank you to Helen Bratby for bringing this book to life through your wonderful design.

To Katherine Stonehouse, my agent, you saw the possibilities in me and catalysed the vision of books to come. You are a great guide through this world of publishing and media.

This book would not have come about without *The Great British Bake-Off*. Thank you to the great team at Love Productions, for selecting me as a contestant: you helped to elevate my skills and gave me a platform to show my baking, personality and culture. To my fellow *Bake-Off* bakers, I learned so much from all of you.

Developing skills and recipes for the book took time and practice. I will be forever grateful to Peter Beeby, David Gold and all my colleagues at Prospectus for giving me the space to flourish.

Along the way all my bakes needed testing and perfecting. Special thanks to the Lewes New School community who challenged my creativity and to my friends Rachel Barnard and David Seidel: you have never missed a chance to drive halfway across town to sample some of my cakes and have supported me every step of the way.

And finally, I want to thank my family: the Poznanskys for their never-ending curiosity and for introducing me to Jewish culture. I feel very grateful to have married into such an inspiring group of people.

And to my parents: Mama, you gave me all your time when I was little, and my love of baking stems from those days making biscuits together around the table. Baba, thank you for letting me mess around with your huge collection of tools, taking me to the brass band and teaching me how to take pride in good craftsmanship. Thank you both for your support and love all along the way.

Thank you to my wonderful son Benjamin, for your excitement whenever I try something new, and for your precise criticism. *Bake-Off* and this book wouldn't have been the same without your input.

To the love of my life, Sophia: thank you for being my wife, partner, friend and coach. You trust me, see ways to develop my creativity which I often miss and you bring me back down to earth whenever I get too lofty. It is a privilege to be by your side, and your contribution to this book is immeasurable.